Emotional Intelligence for Leadership

Improve Your Self-Confidence and Leadership Skills
through Knowledge of Emotions and Human Behavior,
and Enhancing Your Ability to Motivate and Lead People

Larry Newman

Table of Contents

Introduction

Emotional intelligence is the ability to identify, process, and manage one's emotions correctly. Furthermore, one has to accurately identify and influence the feelings of others in his surroundings. In leadership, the role of emotional intelligence gained fame more than a decade ago when an article in Harvard Business Review stated that effective leaders have high emotional intelligence. The skill has developed to be a necessity for one to survive in the business world.

Emotional intelligence comprises of four components.

- Self-awareness

- Social awareness

- Self-management

- Relationship management

Leaders are the center of any organization, which means that they have to possess high levels of emotional intelligence. Failure to have high EQ impacts on performance and employee engagement. High EQ implies that a leader is confident in his abilities, can effectively communicate, and collaborate with different groups of people. Leaders who succeed are those who inspire followers and create an environment that appreciates everyone and promotes innovation.

Successful leaders use emotional intelligence to be effective by leading themselves, others, and the organization. Leaders know that they are not cut from a different cloth- they are imperfect just like anyone else. Therefore, they identify their strengths and weaknesses, work on their strong points, and continually strive to improve on their weak points.

Leaders are aware that they are supposed to lead people, and the right way of influencing others is motivating them. Therefore, a leader studies and understands what motivated other people and what matters to them. After that, a leader provides the resources and necessary support required to make other people great.

Leaders can create and communicate the big picture for an organization to employees, and influence them to support the vision. They help everyone to see that they are essential to the company, and have an indispensable role to play. Thus, they build serious relationships with all stakeholders so that organizational goals are achieved within the required time frame.

Emotional intelligence in leadership is when leaders lead by example. They work with others, and not let others work for them. Leaders who have high EQ are confident, consistent, loyal, and honest. They effectively communicate everything, especially if it involves change. They also make decisions and can self-regulate. They can understand other people's points of view, Because of their ability to read non-verbal communication.

A challenge that affects leadership is when enacting change. At times, leaders can face resistance, and they have to work with everyone so that the change is successful. When experiencing resistance, a leader is supposed to identify the source of resistance, the motivating factors, and do away with it. During the whole process, communication is critical, as unclear communication can make people create fake realities about the situation. At times when all methods have failed, a leader can employ someone else to find the cause of the resistance, and find ways to deal with it.

Emotional intelligence is central to successful relationships, especially in the current workplace, where diversity is celebrated. Therefore, a leader should strive to be emotionally intelligent to create a thriving working environment.

Chapter 1:

Self-Awareness

Experiencing Emotions

There are six basic emotions, which are anger, fear, happiness, surprise, sadness, and disgust. These emotions are all adaptability mechanisms that have evolved and are essential for human survival. They help human beings make quick judgments that are vital for survival. They also help guise necessary behavior. These emotions are directed by the oldest part of the human brain, which is known as the limbic system.

The limbic system consists of the amygdala, hypothalamus, and thalamus. Evolution in human beings has occurred the same way and in the same time span across cultures, which means that emotional reactions are all the same across cultures. Thus, people from different cultures can correctly determine the facial expressions of people from different walks of life.

Some emotions are not determined by the limbic system, which is the oldest part of the brain. Daily experiences are interpreted differently, to create a plethora of emotional reactions. An instance of fear might be explained by the amygdala when someone is suspended from a high place like a building. However, this feeling might be interpreted as something else, for instance, excitement when someone is in a hot air balloon. The amygdala will sense fear, but the experience will determine how the emotional will be interpreted.

Cognitive Appraisal

It is the way the brain interprets sense that accompany emotions. Cognitive appraisal allows human beings to have more emotional experiences, known as secondary emotions. The factor that arouses they determine a significant part of emotional reactions. Thus, the interpretation can either be pleasant or non-pleasant.

An example is when a person finishes a task, they had looked forward to completing for a long time. The person will bask at the moment, and experience an array of secondary emotions such as happiness, contentment, joy, and satisfaction. However, if the same person is unable to finish the project on time, and the friend finishes it within the allocated time, the same person might feel a different set of emotions. Such emotions can be anger, sadness, shame, and resentfulness. The time the emotions last are all dependent on how important the issue was, or how resilient the person is.

Difference Between Primary and Secondary Emotions

Two brain pathways govern the primary and secondary emotions; the fast and slow pathways. The thalamus is responsible for the regulation of this pathway. Fast pathways regulate primary emotions. For instance, when one experiences fear, the thalamus is activated and sends a signal to the amygdala. A person then gets ready to either fly or fight, as a direct response to the fear.

Secondary emotions are controlled by the slow pathway, which is located in the frontal lobe of the cortex. For instance, when a person is jealous that her friend is getting married before her, the emotional process is more complex, as it takes time. Data is moved from the thalamus to the frontal lobe, where it is analyzed. It is processed and integrated and then transferred to the amygdala. There is arousal of emotion, but it is a complicated process that leads to cognitive appraisal. The result is defined; emotions are formulated, and necessary behavior in response to the feelings.

Emotions can be controlled, and as people grow, they get a firm hold on their emotional reactions. Thus, they seem to be not as useful as rational thought. However, emotions are essential in making effective decisions that affect habit and character. In some situations, actions are as a result of logical thinking, whereby the benefits and demerits of a choice are weighed. However, in some instances, the decision-making process is dependent on emotions.

Making emotional decisions comes in handy, especially when the options available present a high level of ambiguity. Thus, proper cognitive analysis is not easy to make in such a situation. It is in such cases that people state that they trust their guilt feeling. At times, decisions made based on emotions are more accurate than those that require rational cognition.

Thus, it is essential for one to correctly identify, and process their emotions, so that they can make proper decisions, especially in instances of high ambiguity and uncertainty.

Theories That Explain the Experience of Emotion

i.   The Cannon-Bard and James- Lange Theory of emotion.

The Canon –Bard theory of emotion states that emotional reaction is conveyed with physiological arousal.

At night, a person can suddenly wake up in the death of night in a panic mode. The fear experienced can be due to the fact that they heard some noises outside, making them think that they were about to be burglarized. Another instance is when a person is walking home, and a bear suddenly appears from the woods. In these instances, the emotional reaction is always physical. The reaction is always either to fly or fight, and this is a critical response system that allows living things to survive in the face of danger. The same response can be applied to different emotions, such as anger, sadness, relentlessness, and love.

When one thinks through such experiences, they might wonder if the arousal occurred before the emotion, or after the emotional reaction. Ideally, it is clear that arousal took place because it is necessary for the physical response to occur.

The experiences of emotion are hypothesized by Cannon and Bard to occur alongside physiological reactions. Thus, one might state that 'I was afraid and my heart started beating like crazy." Therefore, according to this theory, as a person becomes aware of their emotions, their physiological responses also kick in as a response to the feeling.

James Lange holds a slightly different opinion that emotions are as a result of tie arousal that people experience. Therefore, arousal and emotion are two independent entities- they are dependent on each other. Feelings cannot occur without arousal. Therefore, when one is walking in the woods on his way home, and a bear steps in front of his path, he will experience both fear and a beating heart. However, the anxiety and the rapidly beating heart will not occur alongside each other. The fear will be as a result of the beating heart. Thus, any emotional reaction is dependent on the arousal. In an event where the arousal is absent, then the person will not experience the emotional response.

James put it clearly in this statement; we feel sorry because we cry, angry because we strike, afraid because we tremble." Thus, a person with high emotional intelligence will know which arousal to enact, so as to experience a specific set of emotions.

According to this theory, different patterns of arousal create various emotional reactions. It is up to a person to master the various arousal patterns to experience different sets of emotions.

There is evidence that backs of both these theories. The slow and fast emotional pathways research supports the idea that emotions and arousal go hand in hand. Emotional systems in the limbic system become active when something emotional is experienced. These systems quickly create corresponding physiological reactions to accompany emotional stimuli. This process occurs in milliseconds that it seems to human beings that the two processes co-occur.

On the other hand, scientific evidence supports the James- Lange theory, because patients who have spinal injuries have lower instances of arousal. As a result, they also experience lower emotional responses. Thus, it supports the idea that emotional responses are weaker with low arousal. Activity in the amygdala has been studied, and there is evidence to indicate that different patterns of arousal produce mixed emotions.

For instance, people who view angry faces have been shown to produce more activity in the amygdala than those who see joyful faces. Another example is when people have flushed faces when they are embarrassed, and not when they have any other set of emotion.

ii. The two-factor theory of emotion

This theory states that every arousal is the same in every situation experienced. However, emotions are differentiated by the cognitive appraisal process at the source of the arousal. Therefore, emotions are determined by the intensity of the experience, but the type of feeling that will be experienced is dependent on the cognitive appraisal of the situation.

At times, it might be hard for a person to determine the type of emotion they are experiencing, especially at times when they are experiencing high levels of emotions. Therefore, a person can understand what he is experiencing some arousal, but might not be able to place it correctly, and that will affect the cognitive appraisal process.

An example is in romantic relationships, where a person experiences very high levels of arousal. The couple, at times, experiences extreme emotions, and mostly they do not know why they experience such high or intense feelings. Sometimes, they are madly in love, and at other times, they cannot stand to be in the same room.

In situations where a person experiences high levels of arousal, he might not be able to identify the type of emotion that they are feeling correctly. In a relationship, they might not be able to place it as love, hate, or both. All they know is that they are experiencing an emotion, and it is extreme towards their partner.

The trend where people fail to identify and label the source of arousal correctly is known as misattribution of arousal, and it leads to confusion in the type of emotion experienced.

If one thinks about his experiences with different emotions, he might start to wonder which emotions were determined by both arousal and cognition. Therefore, he might be at a conundrum, to identify which emotions were experienced by their feelings, or by their thoughts. The bridge study was done on two study groups of men- one group at a higher bridge, and the other on a lower bridge, indicated that the men were influenced by how they thought they should be feeling, rather than how they were actually feeling.

The theory purports that arousal is the same in all emotions. Thus, emotions can be transferred from one event to the next. For instance, a team can win a tournament, but after the initial celebration, there was a riot in the street. This seems to be a very bizarre reaction to such a positive event. However, this can be explained by the spillover of excitement emotions, to destructive behavior. This principle states that some people might experience other emotions strongly when they are already experiencing another feeling.

Therefore, each of the three theories of emotion explains how emotions are experienced and how they are identified. In the first theory, emotions and arousal occur hand in hand, and the reaction is usually swift. Therefore, in a social situation, it is responsible for fast responses and can be useful in solving condition which offers high levels of uncertainty and ambiguity.

The Lange theory states that emotions are weak without feelings, and there is some scientific evidence to prove it. There is also proof that different patterns if arousal is responsible for different sets of emotions.

The two-factor model states that the same patterns of arousal can result in different sets of emotions. It all depends on the situation and the cognition. Ideally, most people react according to how they feel they should respond, and not how they ought to have responded.

Communicating Emotion

People experience emotions intrinsically and express these emotions to people. On the same note, people learn about the feelings of other people by observing them. Communication is a process that has to be continually learned and is highly adaptive. It has evolved, but there is some basis of communication, especially when it comes to nonverbal communication that is universal across cultures.

The ability to correctly identify and communicate one's emotion is dependent on someone's emotional intelligence. People who are emotionally intelligent can correctly identify process and communicate their feelings. They can also correctly identify and process the emotions of other people.

Nonverbal communication involves any form of communication that occurs without the use of words. Therefore, it consists of the application of tone, gait, posture, touch, and facial expressions. People can often tell the emotions of other people by studying nonverbal communication.

There is no universal nonverbal communication, and different cultures have different signs they use. However, the face is the most basic mode of communication. The feedback hypothesis purports that the movement of the 43 muscles found in the face can lead to different emotions.

Behavior is both influenced and influences a person's affective state. For instance, a person can smile because he is happy, but he can also be happy because he is smiling. Another example is a person might stand up straight because he is proud, or he might be proud because he is standing up straight.

i. Take emotional temperature

One way for one to be aware of their emotions is to take their emotional temperature. This means that one has to note down the feelings he is feeling, which one is most prominent, and when they started identifying this emotion. Each feeling should be described in detail, and a person should not be afraid to push so that the answers are not vague. This is not to be done for the unpleasurable emotions only; they are also to be done for the pleasure bale ones too so that a person knows what makes them happy.

ii. Identify stressors

Identify the reasons why the feelings are triggered. Find out the events going on in their daily life, and pay close attention to events, dreams, that one has no control over, and might affect their everyday life. At times, the things one refuses to pay attention to might be the reason for their downfall, because the feeling of having no control is enough to elicit an emotional reaction.

At times, the answer to such questions might not be clear. A person might say that they do not know how they feel. The directive to take in such a situation is to examine daily life. It will help bring out behavior that would not have been recognized easily. Look for patterns in the relationship one has, and identify what they might be communicating.

Be on the lookout for judgment. Identify areas where one judges himself, and what type of judgment he passes. In life, all events generate some reaction. A person can decide what feelings to respond to. However, they do not have control over their feelings, and cannot decide whether to feel or not to feel. It is a person's responsibility to identify these feelings and process them well.

Emotions that are denied, or made to be small, do not go away. Instead, they grow bigger in size. Therefore, it is a bad idea to dismiss feelings. Instead, one should correctly identify them and acknowledge them. If it is hard to process them, then they should talk to someone else, because in this case, they will be recognized and processed.

Often, people are scared to face emotions because of the consequences. It is essential to understand that confronting a feeling is different from acting on it. The response is dependent on how well a person acknowledges the emotion.

Chapter 2:

Self-Regulation

Self-regulation entails regulating an individual's actions, sentiments, and feelings while seeking long-term objectives. Emotionally, self-regulation implies the capacity to handle disturbing sentiments and desires. Additionally, it shows the skill to encourage yourself after displeasure and to behave in a manner consistent with your standards.

Growth

The skill to self-regulate like a grown-up begins during an individual's development at babyhood. Learning self-regulation is a significant ability that kids acquire for both social links and emotional development.

In a perfect circumstance, a child who shows irritability develops into a baby who understands how to accept itchy sentiments without hurling a fit. Additionally, the child grows-up capable of controlling impulses and behaves based on painful sentiments. Conversely, adulthood echoes the skill to face emotional, communal, and cognitive intimidation in the surroundings with endurance and care.

Significance

Self-regulation entails seeking a break between sentiments and deeds. Children frequently fail with these conduct and grown-ups, as well.

It is simple to perceive how deprivation of self-regulation shall bring troubles in life. Children who shout or beat other kids because of irritation shall not be accepted, among others, and might experience scolding in educational centers. A grown-up with deprived self-regulation abilities might need self-assurance and a sense of worth and have problems dealing with pressure and annoyance. Regularly, this may be shown as rage or nervousness, and in cruel situations, it might be established as a psychological problem.

Self-regulation is significant because it permits you to behave according to your standards or social principles and to communicate in a good way. If you adore educational accomplishment, it shall permit you to revise other than slacking prior to an examination. If you enjoy serving other people, it will let you assist a co-worker with an assignment, irrespective of how you are stretched with the time limit.

In its fundamental structure, self-regulation permits people to come back from disappointment and remain peaceful with stress. The two skills will take an individual through daily existence, better than other abilities.

General Troubles

How does trouble regarding self-regulation grow? It might begin initially as a baby being abandoned. Babies, who are not protected, or not sure if their requirements shall be fulfilled, might have problems regarding self-regulation.

Eventually, a baby, youngster, or a grown-up might have difficulties with self-regulation, as this talent was not natured either during the early days or as a result of deprivation of tactics for handling complex sentiments. When not checked, this might result in severe problems such as psychological problems and dangerous acts such as drug consumption.

Useful Policies

If self-regulation is subsequently vital, why were the majority of us not at all trained tactics for applying this ability? Frequently, caregivers, instructors, and other grown-ups imagine that kids will develop out of the paroxysm stage. However, this is right for the majority part; all family and grown-ups might profit from acquiring real tactics for self-regulation.

Mindfulness

In emotional intelligence, Mindfulness entails the nurturing of minute-to-minute consciousness through realistic practices like deep inhalation. Inhalation assists with self-regulation by permitting an individual to wait for satisfaction and handle sentiments. Several reviews of research journals showed that mindfulness influences awareness, which later assisted in controlling unconstructive influence and decision-making execution.

Cognitive Reassessment

Cognitive reassessment is an approach that might be applied to develop self-regulation capabilities. The cognitive reassessment tactic entails altering your thinking models. According to research, the embrace of cognitive re-evaluation is linked with lesser unhelpful effects and a greater helpful result. Cognitive reassessment means opinion regarding a circumstance in an adaptive manner, instead of one that is expected to boost unhelpful feelings. Several other helpful policies for self-regulation comprise approval and difficulty solving. Contrary, unsupportive policies that individuals occasionally use involve evading, interruption, repression, and upsetting.

Character of Self-Regulators

The reimbursements of self-regulation are many. Generally, individuals who are proficient at self-regulating see excellence in others and perceive challenges as excellent chances. Additionally, they uphold genuine communication, are evident regarding their purpose, and behave per their principles. Similarly, they put forward their most exceptional try, keep moving during tricky moments, stay flexible, and adjust to circumstances. They as well take charge of events if required, and might relax if displease and be encouraged if feeling distressed.

Practicing

People doubtless think that it looks magnificent to be exceptional at self-regulating. However, they do not distinguish how to develop their abilities.

In kids, caregivers might assist grow self-regulation by using a schedule. Practice assists kids in discovering what to anticipate and make it simple for children to feel happy. If children behave in a manner that does not show self-regulation, disregard their desires, by letting them hang around if they disrupt a discussion.

The first phase of practicing self-regulation is identifying that everybody has an option in how to respond to circumstances. Distinguishing that in each circumstance, people have three major preferences: move toward, evading, and assault. Though it might appear as although people's selection of deeds is out of their hands, it is not. Their feelings might influence them more toward a single pathway, but they are better than those sentiments.

The following phase is to be conscious of the temporary thoughts. Do people think of escaping from tricky circumstances? Do people consider shouting out in rage at somebody who has upset them? People should watch their bodies to get a hint regarding how they feel if it is not instantly apparent to them. For instance, a quickly escalating heart might be a symbol that an individual is going into a status of fury or a fright assault.

People should Begin to reinstate stability by centering on their exceptionally held standards, instead of those temporary feelings. Subsequently, act in a manner that concurs with self-regulation.

The Skill of Self-Regulation

Study consistently demonstrates that self-regulation skill is required for dependable emotional well-being. Behaviorally, self-regulation is the skill to act in your best interest, consistent with your values. Emotionally, self-regulation is the skill to compose yourself when you are distressed and cheer yourself up when you are hurt.

If, like the majority of us, you might stand to develop self-regulation skills, an excellent point to begin is an understanding of the biology and purpose of emotions and purposely feelings. Self-regulation is a single type of skill. It permits children to manage their feelings, behavior, and body faction when they are faced with circumstances that are hard to handle. Besides, it allows them to do that while still alert and paying attention.

That implies that children recognize how to figure out that they require calming themselves down when they get disappointed. They are flexible when expectations adjust, and they might oppose giving in to irritating outbursts. This ability develops over time. That is why it is common to notice a four-year-old having an outburst, but not a twelve-year-old. If a twelve-year-old frequently has a bad temper, he or she likely has difficulty with self-regulation.

The Skill of Shifting Attention and Focus

Focused attention is the skill to respond to a particular stimulus. In the early stages, people shall respond to prompt such as hurting and cold but might not respond to stimuli such as seeing a loved one and hearing his/her name being called.

Sustained attention is the skill to sustain concentration on a mission. Measuring sustained attention might be for a time a person may attend to duty without losing focus or taking a pause. Examples of sustained concentration comprise reading for a period without taking a break; having a discussion without looking at other issues; or functioning on a dull, recurring duty.

Selective attention is the skill to concentrate on vital details and screen out inconsequential information such as exterior distractions or internal distractions. Examples of selective attention comprise revising while playing music in the background, having a discussion in a noisy neighborhood, and baring arriving visual information while looking for items to purchase.

Alternating attention is the skill to switch concentration from one duty to another or one element of the chore to another. Instances of the shift of attention comprise working on a laptop, answering the telephone and going back to functioning on the computer, listening to a lecture, and writing notes.

Divided attention is the skill to concentrate on more than a single duty or parts of an assignment at the same time. Instances of divided attention comprise taking care of the child while cooking; listening to the radio while riding; pushing the handcart while looking at the shelve for a product; cooking two meals at the same time.

Negative Emotions and Their Impact

Anger, irritation, panic, and other negative emotions are all elements of the human experience. They lead to stress and are frequently perceived as emotions to be avoided. However, they may be healthy for us to practice as well. A more robust approach is to handle them without rejecting them, and there are many reasons for this.

Managing Negative Emotions

The thought of handling negative emotions is a difficult one. It does not imply avoiding feeling them. It, as well, does not imply letting these unconstructive emotions wreak mayhem on your life, your affairs, and your anxiety levels. Unmanaged rage, for example, may compel us to demolish relationships if we permit it to.

Managing unhelpful emotions is about accepting that we feel them, influencing why we are reacting this way, and letting ourselves obtain the messages that they are conveying to us before we let them go.

Effects of Negative Emotions

Anger, fright, resentment, irritation, and nervousness are emotional conditions that several people experience frequently but try to evade. Besides, this is comprehensible because they are intended to make us painful. These unenthusiastic emotional states might create extra stress on the body and the brain, which is painful but also might lead to health matters if the stress becomes persistent or devastating. No one likes to feel painful, so it is usual to want to flee these feelings, and the threats of unmanaged stress are genuine. However, there is a feeling that individuals sometimes have that these sentiments will last eternally or that the feelings themselves are the difficulty.

Frequently, these feelings are valuable because they may also send us a communication. Anger and nervousness, for instance, show that something requires to change, and possibly that our well-being has been endangered. Fear is a plea to boost your level of security. Resentment stimulates us to modify something in an affair. Depressing emotions are there to notify us that something requires to adjust and to inspire us to make that alteration.

Temper Negative Responses

A bad temper might also be a sudden unfortunate or negative reaction that somebody has in a definite situation. An irregular angered reaction does not essentially indicate a correct bad temper. A complete diagnosis needs the appearance of behavioral and sentimental movements, along with bodily and emotional indicators that also happen often. It might be anger that plays a role; there might also be a difficulty with managing anger confidently.

Some triggers might cause rage or irritability, physical and mental. These may be worry, busy occupation, and lifestyles, as well as devastating family, social, and economic errands.

Some of the bodily causes of a terrible temper comprise sleep deficiency, diabetes, and flu.

Identify the Triggers and discover Solutions

Particularly if you have taken a magazine, it is simple to establish the things in each day's life that might trigger an awful mood in you. From matters as simple as intense or controversial discussion topics lead you to annoyance, then it is good to shun them as much as possible. If other people happen to bring them up, you might recognize that you are like ablaze and begin to force yourself away once you start to get involved intensely. If you recognize that take a deep inhalation or walking away shall calm you, then it is fine to compel yourself to do so.

Controlling Negative Emotions

For individual and professional affairs to thrive, negative emotions must be handled cautiously, so that a firm foundation of confidence and respect might be built. The following are steps to take while controlling negative emotions.

Look Frankly at Yourself

Mitigating or rationalizing pessimistic emotions will not serve you fine. While it might be tricky to do in the heat of the minute, you require looking at how you are reacting to circumstances with total sincerity. Characteristically, people are incapable of acknowledging that their behavior was shocking. They could rather rationalize their anger, fright, hatred, conceit, stubbornness, and bitterness than admit that it does not help them or other people. Step back from this inflexible wish to be right, and see how your emotional reactions are upsetting those around you.

Communicate Constructively

The expression of downbeat emotions is the trademark of the failure to communicate wisely. If events happen that trigger your unenthusiastic emotions, you require reflecting, deliberating, and exploring what is at the cause of that outburst. If another individual's behavior was unsuitable, you must find a way to speak to him or her constructively. Discarding on other people is unhelpful.

Find a Vent

Filling your sentiments is no way to handle them. You require respecting your bodily processes. If you feel like setting off or collapse, then you might require doing that. You must find channels to do it correctly. Finding a vent will appear different for diverse people. Some individuals might need to take a walk or a bathe, maybe get an excellent night's sleep, or work out to blow off steam. You require discovering what functions for you.

Practice Self-Care

Frequently negative sentiments are the side effect of not taking care of the body. It is as if negative power builds up in your mind and bodily processes over time. When that is the situation, it comes out finally. With good self-care, your globe view might take on a completely new value. Self-care might include a standard massage, exercise, correct diet, and appropriate meditation. It is astonishing how small exercise is required to make a huge difference. 15 to 20 minutes a day in the gym may do the trick. A pair of dumbbells at home might be quite enough.

Managing Anger

Anger is a natural, healthy feeling. However, it may occur out of proportion to its prompt. In these situations, the emotion might obstruct a person's decision-making, break relationships, and or else cause damage. Learning to manage anger might limit the emotional harm.

Anger is a familiar response to annoying or intimidating experiences. It may also be a secondary reaction to sadness, isolation, or fright. In some situations, the emotion might seem to occur from nowhere.

Feeling annoyed often and to a great degree can influence affairs and a person's mental well-being and value of life. Restraining and storing up rage may also have a destructive and lasting consequence.

Anger management entails a range of abilities that might help with recognizing the indicators of anger and effectively managing the triggers. It requires an individual to recognize anger at an early phase and to express their desires while remaining peaceful and in control. Managing fury does not entail holding it in or evading associated feelings. Coping with annoyance is an acquired ability, and almost anybody may learn to manage the emotions with time, patience, and commitment.

When anger is harmfully affecting an affair, leading to aggressive behavior, a person might benefit from consulting a psychological health expert or attending an anger management institution. However, there are early, immediate practices to try. Several people find that they might resolve these problems without seeking specialized assistance.

Working Effectively with Difficult People

Difficult individuals do exist at workplaces and other places as well. They come in every range, and no place of work is without them. How complicated a person is for you to handle depends on your self-respect, your self-assurance, and your professional audacity at work.

Dealing with sophisticated individuals is more comfortable when the individual is just normally obnoxious or when the action affects more than one individual. Handling them is harder when they are attacking you, silently criticizing you, or disheartening your professional involvement.

Complicated people come in every imaginable variety. Some speak persistently and never listen. Others must constantly have the last expression. Some colleagues fail to keep promises. Others condemn anything that they did not produce. Difficult colleague competes with you for authority, privilege, and the attention; some go excessively far in courting the manager's positive judgment to your disadvantage.

Develop Self-Awareness

You might learn all the approaches to handle sophisticated persons; however, learning to handle your own feelings is vital. This is where self-awareness chips in, and it will be the game changer once you understand it.

To be self-aware, you require practicing detecting your feelings, judgment, and behavior. Identify your prompt and the things that difficult individuals do to get under your skin. Some individuals find it useful to begin keeping a small notepad or periodical with them and recording things as they emerge.

Be Assertive and Set Boundaries

A self-confident person takes full accountability for herself and her behavior. When a difficult person infringes on her borders, she does not request to be accountable for that person's behaviors.

Listen Carefully

Give the complex person a chance to conclude without disrupting. Ask descriptive questions if bemused, and use rephrasing and mirroring to verify the correctness of hearing.

Give Feedback

There is an occasion when a difficult individual has to be notified his deeds are affecting you and is no longer bearable.

The Ability to Heal

Emotional healing is a procedure. It calls for several abilities. You will require some control over your concentration, the ability to attend with the emotions you notice, and the skill to let go of them. Breath-work practice is frequently deployed. It is supportive, if not necessary. You will also require the awareness to scrutinize the thoughts in your mind and see that they are not right. These are all forms of mindfulness and consciousness practices that are united for emotional healing to succeed.

Be Alert of Your Emotions

Getting true with yourself and permitting your mind to operate through any sentiment, you might feel bubbling up from time to time is so significant. As a past feeling-stuffer, people understand how strenuous it is to pretend to be cheerful all of the time. They also know it is impractical and not sustainable.

Stop Pity Party

To cure, it is imperative to modify your mindset around curing. Throwing yourself a disappointment party is a simple way to stumble, sulk around, and finds momentary relief; however, this does not produce any permanent results.

Avoid Revenge

Although seeking revenge is frequently advisable by many, living your life thinking about revenge on whatever offended you might not help. Seeking revenge might not help, but it adds more pain to the person seeking payback. A key step in healing yourself is releasing the natural intuition to seek revenge or source pain to whatever it is that impair you in the first place.

Managing Stress

There are a set of techniques intended to assist people to deal more successfully with anxiety. The techniques analyzing the exact stressors and suggest helpful actions to reduce their effects. The action-oriented method permits you to take action and adjust the traumatic situation.

Below are some of the approaches deployed in managing stress.

Be Assertive

Clear and effective communication is essential to being **assertive**. When we are confident, we may inquire for what we desire or want, and clarify what is troubling us. The essence is doing this fairly and stably whilst still having an understanding for others. Once you spot what you require to communicate, you may stand up for yourself and be positive in altering the traumatic situation.

Time Management

If we allow stress, our days shall eat us. Before we recognize it, the months have become devastatingly demanding. When we prioritize and arrange our responsibilities, we produce a less worrying and more pleasant life.

Create Boundaries

Boundaries are the inner set of rules that we create for ourselves. Boundaries draw what behaviors we shall and will not acknowledge. Boundaries also indicate how much time and room we require from others, and what choices we have.

Diet and Exercise

You have heard it previously; you are what you consume. Be watchful of having a reasonable and well diet. Making uncomplicated diet changes, such as lowering your alcohol, and sugar ingestion is an accepted method of **reducing nervousness**.

Talk it Out

Do not hold it all in. Speak to somebody close to you regarding your fears or the things stressing you. Sharing uncertainties may slash them in half, and offer you an opportunity to laugh at potentially illogical circumstances.

The Role of Self-Regulatory in Security Sector

Self-regulation in the defense markets is in evolution: several countries question its usefulness in today's difficult environment, while others know its potential to assist in the expansion of economies across boundaries. Although conventional forms of self-regulation deserve re-examination, the successful use of front-line monitors, such as self-regulatory institutes, offers huge potential in our unified monetary markets.

The Role of Self-Regulation in Leadership

Leaders who show good self-regulation are capable to control their emotions and answers to situations and other individuals. They do not have heated outbursts or make sudden judgments. They are sincere and their deed is in line with their principles. They are adjustable, capable of working with diverse people in different circumstances. Experts who understand how to self-regulate are able to glance at the whole picture rationally and put the circumstances in perspective. They are considerate. They do not put blame, dwell on circumstances, give up, or consider themselves a casualty. They guide by example.

Chapter 3:

Acquiring Emotional Intelligence

Emotional intellect is the component in every one of us that is indefinable. It influences how we handle behavior, navigate societal complexities, and make individual decisions that attain a positive outcome. Emotional intelligence comprises of four fundamental skills that are grouped into two main competencies: personal skill and social ability.

Personal competence comprises of your self-management and self-awareness skills, which dwells more on you separately than on your communications with other individuals. Personal skill is your aptitude to stay alert of your emotions and handle your actions and tendencies.

Self-Awareness is your skill to correctly perceive your feelings and stay sensitive to them as they occur. Self-Management is your skill to use the consciousness of your emotions to remain flexible and positively control your behavior. Social competence comprises of your social alertness and relationship management abilities. Social ability is your skill to appreciate other people's moods, actions, and motives to develop the value of your relationships. Social-Awareness is your skill to correctly notice emotions in other people and know what is truly going on. Relationship Management is your skill to use alertness of your emotions and the others' feelings to manage communications effectively.

Emotional intellect taps into a basic element of human actions that are different from your intelligence. There is no identified connection between intelligent quotient and emotional intelligence. You plainly cannot predict emotional intellect based on how elegant someone is. Intelligence is your skill to study, and it is equal at age ten as it is at age forty. Emotional intellect, on the other hand, is a flexible collection of skills that might be acquired and developed with practice. Several people are naturally emotionally intelligent than others. However, people might develop high emotional intelligence even if they were not born with it.

Individuality is the final piece of the dilemma. Personality is an established style that describes each of us. Personality is the outcome of liking, such as the love toward extroversion or introversion. Conversely, like intelligent quotient, personality cannot be used to guess emotional intelligence. In addition, like intelligent quotient, personality is firm over a lifetime and does not vary. Intelligent quotient, emotional intellect, and personality each cover exceptional ground and assist in clarifying what makes a person functional.

The interaction between your emotional and sane brainpower is the physical basis of emotional intelligence.

The lane for emotional intellect starts in mind, at the spinal cord. Your main senses penetrate here and must move to the front of your mind before you may think rationally about your practice. However, initially, they move through the limbic structure, the position where emotions are produced. Therefore, we have an emotional response to proceedings before our rational brain is able to connect. Emotional intelligence wants efficient communication between the lucid and emotional location of the brain.

Plasticity is the word neurologists apply to explain the brain's ability to adjust. Your mind grows fresh connections as you discover new abilities. The alteration is gradual, as your mind cells develop fresh connections to speed the competence of new abilities acquired.

Influence of Emotional Intelligence Your Job

How much of an influence does emotional intelligence have on your professional accomplishment? It is an influential way to focus your power on one path with a tremendous outcome. Several researches were carried out regarding emotional intelligence together with other significant workplace abilities. These studies established that emotional intelligence is the biggest predictor of performance; explaining a higher percentage of success in all sorts of jobs. Additionally, your emotional intelligence is the basis for a multitude of decisive skills, and it influences most everything you speak and do daily.

Of all the individuals studied at occupation, research established that 90 percent of top contributors are also excellent in emotional intelligence. On the other region, just 20 percent of bottom contributors are excellent in emotional intelligence. You might be a good performer without emotional intelligence, but the chances are slender.

Naturally, individuals with a superior degree of emotional intelligence make more money as opposed to people with a small degree of emotional intellect. The connection between emotional intelligence and earnings is so straight that every point increase in emotional intelligence adds extra dollars to a yearly salary. These conclusions hold true for individuals in all industries, at all heights, in every section of the globe. We have not yet been capable of finding an occupation in which performance and payment are not tied directly to emotional intelligence

Emotional intelligence continues to be an ever more popular ability to have in the professional globe. Many might be wondering why emotional intellect continues to boost in importance between peers in an evolving place of work. Simply put, emotional intelligence is not a movement. Major businesses have compiled numerical proof that workers with emotional intelligence unquestionably influence the bottom line. Businesses with workers that have excellent levels of emotional intelligence perceive a major rise in total sales and production.

In an aggressive workplace, increasing your emotional intelligence skills is fundamental to your professional accomplishment. Below are methods to boost your emotional intelligence.

Use an Assertive Technique of Communication

Self-assured communicating goes a long way to earning admiration without coming across as too violent or too submissive. Emotionally bright people identify how to communicate their judgment and needs in a straight manner while still respecting other people.

Answer Instead of Reacting to Disagreement

During cases of conflict, emotional explosions and feelings of rage are common. The emotionally gifted person recognizes how to remain calm during traumatic situations. They do not make spontaneous decisions that may lead to even bigger troubles. They know that in times of disagreement, the objective is a resolution, and they create a conscious alternative to focus on ensuring that their behavior and words are in **configuration with that.**

Use Active Listening Abilities

In discussions, emotionally smart people pay attention to clarity instead of waiting for their time to talk. They make sure they know what is said before reacting. They as well pay attention to the nonverbal information of a discussion. This stops misunderstandings, permits the listener to reply correctly, and shows respect for the individual they are talking with.

Be Motivated

Emotionally smart people are vibrant, and their approach motivates other people. They set objectives and are resilient in the face of tests.

Uphold a Positive Attitude

Do not undervalue the influence of your attitude. A downbeat attitude effortlessly contaminates others if a person permits it to. Emotionally bright people have alertness of the tempers of those around them and watch their attitude consequently. They recognize what they require to have a fine day and an optimistic attitude. This might include having a superior meal, engaging in prayer or deliberation during the daytime, or keeping constructive quotes at their desk or laptop.

Apply Self-Awareness

Emotionally smart people are self-aware and insightful. They are conscious of their feelings and understand how they might affect other people. They also notice others' feelings and body language and utilize that information to improve their communication abilities.

Accept Critique

A significant part of mounting your emotional intelligence is to be capable of taking critique. Instead of getting defensive, high emotional intelligent individuals seek to know where the criticism is coming from. They also understand how it is touching others or their personal actions, and how they might constructively settle the issue.

Empathize with Other People

Emotionally bright people understand how to empathize. They know that understanding is a characteristic that shows emotional power, not weakness. Understanding assists them in relating to others on a fundamental human height. It unlocks the door for mutual admiration and understanding between individuals with differing judgments and situations.

Use Leadership Skills

Emotionally gifted people have outstanding leadership abilities. They have superior standards for themselves and show an example for others to copy. They take a program and have great verdict making and investigative abilities. This allows for a superior and more industrious level of performance in life and at the place of work.

Be Friendly and Sociable

Emotionally bright people come off as friendly. They laugh and give off an encouraging charisma. They use suitable social skills based on their association with whomever they are talking with. They have vast interpersonal skills and understand how to communicate unmistakably, whether the message is spoken or nonverbal.

Several of these skills might seem to be best matched for those who know basic human psychology. Whereas high emotional intelligent skills might come more effortlessly to naturally compassionate people, anyone might enlarge them. Less compassionate people must practice being self-aware and aware of how they interrelate with others. By exploiting these procedures, you will be well on your track to an increase in your emotional intellect level.

How to Become More Emotionally Intelligent

Understandably, that we are all emotionally bright, but we require taking more time to self-assess and work on our feelings. As with everything, it takes practice, but even little steps might make a huge difference. Greatly as you might regularly train your biceps or any other muscle for that subject, you require practicing working on your skills so that they get better.

Admittedly, when we look at heads in a number of flourishing companies, it is clear that all these heads have shown high levels of the components of emotional intellect. It is vital to bear in mind that these are a variety of skills. Overall, women tend to have a superior emotional understanding on average: sensing how somebody is in the moment, managing relationships between people and crowds. The analysis on the link between emotional intelligence and headship is that there are variations between women and men in this field, but as people grow, they pick up expertise in the area they require.

Influence of Emotional Intelligence at Work

Each day we create emotionally charged choices. We think plan A is superior to plan B, and we sometimes make selections based on our emotions. When we know the basis of these emotions, particularly when functioning in a group, we are more at attuned to everyone. With globalization, emotional intelligence is more important than ever when co-workers are cross-cultural and universal, increasing the difficulty of exuding emotions. Emotional intellect in the workplace comes down to accepting, expressing and organization, excellent relationships and solving problems under stress.

Importance of Emotional Intellect at Work

A lot of people who have researched leadership indicate that self-awareness makes it easy to know your desires. Self-awareness helps in knowing the possible reactions if certain proceedings occurred, thereby facilitating the assessment of alternative answers.

The emotional intelligence to be successful, it has to begin with yourself. You may not refine or improve other people's well-being, development, and sense of self without first accepting how you function on an emotional level. What differentiates leaders is frequently their level of emotional intelligence. Besides, those abilities assist in expanding a successful workplace.

Emotionally Intelligent Leaders

Emotionally intelligent leaders promote safe environments, where workers feel happy to take risks, propose ideas, and voice their judgment. In such secure environments, working collaboratively is not an objective, but it is woven into the executive culture as a whole.

When a director is emotionally smart, they might utilize emotions to drive the business forward. Leaders frequently have the accountability of effecting any needed changes in the organization. In addition, if they are conscious of others' likely emotional reactions to these adjustments, they are able to sketch and prepare the finest ways to make them.

Additionally, emotionally bright leaders do not take things individually and are capable of forging ahead with policies without worrying about the influence on their egos. Individual disputes between leaders and staff are one of the commonest obstacles to productivity in several workplaces.

Leaders with Low Emotional Intelligence

Leadership is a stressful authorization; being accountable for the fate of several people might take its toll. Heads that have low emotional intelligence tend to struggle during traumatic circumstances. The struggle is because of the failure to deal with their emotions, and this may manifest as verbal assault and physical violence.

The struggle might produce an even more worrying environment, where employees are trying to stop the next outburst from occurring. This frequently has devastating effects on production and team cohesion because the workers stay too troubled by this fright to focus on job and bond.

Not being emotionally clever hinders teamwork within the organization. When a leader reacts inappropriately, most of their workers tend to feel anxious about contributing their thoughts and suggestions, for panic of how the leader will answer.

Conversely, a leader who needs emotional intelligence does not essentially lash out at their workers. Not being emotionally smart can also imply incapacity to address circumstances that could be loaded with emotion. Most heads deal with disagreement, and a leader who is not informed about others' emotions shall regularly have a tricky time recognizing disagreement and effectively resolving it.

Emotional Intellect Assists Leaders to Adjust

Leaders also need to adjust to changing situations in their workplaces or in their roles and those of their group members. In addition, Emotional intelligence shall allow an individual to be more flexible in society. Emotional intelligence is a fundamental leadership ability. Moreover, for a leader to be successful, they should be masterful and constructively handling their relationships. Being the head of people is to have a very significant relationship with those individuals.

This is not to state that emotional intelligence is sufficient to get you to that leadership point in your job. You shall still require professional familiarity and experience. However, it implies that if you take a leadership position and have a superior degree of emotional intellect, you will possibly be more successful. Because feelings are always in fluctuation, adaptability is paramount to being an exceptional leader.

Great Leaders Develop Their Organizations

When it comes to the place of work, and particularly business, the bottom line is vital, and managers and managers are held responsible for accomplishment and collapse. Researchers collected direct reports from workers regarding their leaders from different business and found several key personalities most flourishing leaders possess.

There is a balanced rise in worker satisfaction with the growth of good leaders. Poor leaders' workers have poor job fulfillment, and good leaders' workers are much more committed and pleased with their job. Some of those techniques include focusing on chances and possibilities instead of troubles, celebrating victorious events, being inquisitive regarding individual employees' profession aspirations and assisting in accomplishing them.

Even more appealing is that when you have a good leader, they may double a company's earnings. Most of us would think that emotional intelligence might not have to do much with a business's bottom line. However, when a company has a good manager who possesses and uses effective emotional intelligence, your business will significantly benefit

Phases of Acquiring Emotional Intelligence

Insight

Any learning begins when we are conscious that there is an element in us, which requires changing or improving, and we are prepared to make those adjustments happen. Emotional intelligence has five elements in it.

Learning emotional intelligence begins with gaining insight into which feature of emotional intelligence we must work on. Some of us might have solid social abilities but lack self-regulation while others might be superior in motivation but underprivileged in self-regulation. The learning procedure starts with the knowledge of which element of emotional intelligence to develop first.

Assessment

The following step is attempting to steps where we stand on each of the emotional intelligence elements. In addition, emotional intelligence tests are widely accessible online. If you are looking for training in a professional context, there will be resources provided to you for examining your emotional intelligence.

Here are a few **measurements** that we can take to assess our emotional intelligence. The scores in each of them are pointers of whether or not we require to learn emotional abilities, and where do we stand as an emotionally conscious human being.

Training

Evaluation opens us to a variety of options for selection. Depending on what section of emotional intelligence we require to work on, we might decide what kind of training might suit us the best. For instance, low achievement in motivational and communal communication features may be improved by organizational guidance.

Low Emotional Intelligence

Low emotional intellect is a predicament that may sway a large range of communal affairs. Several professionals propose that emotional intelligence might be more significant than the intelligence quotient to determine accomplishment in life.

Emotional intelligence might have a cardinal influence on how we interrelate with other people. Occasionally workmates, managers, acquaintances, relatives, and other associates may have difficulties with deprived emotional abilities, which form social circumstances hard and loaded with anxiety. In other instances, it may be your emotional aptitude abilities, which calls for a slight job.

A person's intensity of emotional intellect is frequently perceived as their emotional intelligence quotient. Below are a number of the standard indicators of short emotional intellect.

Getting in Countless Quarrels

You possibly know somebody who constantly appears to get into fights with other people. Acquaintances, relatives, workmates, and casual guests find themselves engaged in a heated discussion with these confrontational persons. Since small emotional intelligence, people find it hard to recognize the sentiments of others; they regularly get themselves quarreling devoid of bearing in mind how other people are suffering.

Not Accepting Other People's Feelings

Low emotional intelligence individuals are entirely unaware of the thoughts of other persons. They do not *understand* that their partner may be heated with them or that their workmates are aggravated. Besides, they as well feel bothered that other individuals anticipate them to understand how they are thinking. Feelings, generally, frustrate citizens with little emotional intelligence.

Assuming that Others Are Excessively Sensitive

Individuals who are stumpy in emotional intelligence might break jokes in the wrong period. For instance, they may joke at a memorial service or after a disastrous episode. If other people respond to the comic story, the short emotional intelligent being might feel like other people are responsive. These persons have trouble accepting the feelings of other people, so it is diminutive doubt why they are incapable of understanding the arousing nature after such proceedings.

Not Listening to Others

Low emotional intellect individuals think that they are right and shall defend their stance with enormous dynamism, yet reject to pay attention to what other people have to state. This is principally correct if other individuals are not in acceptance of how the person does not realize what other people are undergoing. They are frequently unenthusiastic and excessively in disagreement with other individual's sentiments.

Shifting the Blame

Persons with small emotional intellect have a small perception of how their emotions may result in troubles. If their plans go incorrect, their initial intuition is to fault other people. They regularly fault distinctiveness of the circumstances or the actions of other persons for their choices. They may propose that they did not have any other option for what occurred and that people do not understand their circumstances. The affinity of not taking blame frequently allows them to feel bitter and badly treated.

Unable to Deal with Emotionally Altered Circumstances

Strong feelings, whether theirsor of others, are hard to understand for people with small emotional intellect. These persons will frequently run from these circumstances to shun dealing with the arousing arguments. Concealing their correct sentiments from other people is well known.

Unexpected Emotional Outbursts

The skill of regulating sentiments is one of the five essential aspects of emotional intellect. Persons with small emotional intelligence often find it hard to comprehend and handle their feelings. They may have an unpredicted arousing explosion that appears exaggerated and unmanageable.

Unable to Maintain Friends

Since small emotional intelligent citizens repeatedly appear as rude and unsympathetic, they have trouble keeping friends. Generally, friendships entail sharing of sentiments, empathy, and emotional backup, all of which low emotional intelligent persons struggle to uphold.

Lack of Understanding

Since persons with small emotional intellect do not know the feelings of other people, they have a small understanding of other people's sentiments. They do not comprehend what other people are undergoing, so it is impractical for them to know what other people are experiencing.

Deprived emotional intellect might cause havoc in several regions of an individual's existence. School, occupation, relatives, companionship, and passionate affiliation are a few segments where an individual with small emotional intelligence will encounter key troubles.

Emotional intelligence is necessary for excellent interpersonal communication. Several experts believe that this skill is more vital in determining life accomplishment than IQ alone. Luckily, there are things that you might do to enhance your own communal and emotional intelligence. Accepting emotions might be the key to good relationships, enhanced well-being, and stronger communication abilities.

Chapter 4:

Developing a Positive Emotional Focus

Effective leaders know the significance of positive emotions in their personal lives and leadership roles. When someone goes seeking for personal growth advice, the professionals aim to make the person feel and concentrate on achieving positive emotions in all circumstances. We do what we do because we look forward to becoming happier, more optimistic, and more outgoing in the process, or as a result of it. Positive emotions emanate from positive emotions and produce more positive emotions. Negative emotions on the other hand result from negative emotions.

The Merits of Positive Emotional Focus

Keeping a positive emotional outlook helps to broaden and deepen one's attention and focus. This is a consequence of the state of mental equilibrium that the person enjoys which makes them open-minded and willing and patient in their undertakings. This works by itself also to effectively build their personal resources physically, intellectually, socially, and psychologically necessary for handling life issues.

Emotionally focused persons also enjoy an increased degree and scope of cognition. One sees more interconnections in the world, becomes more flexible in their thinking and sees more relations and integrations in thoughts and ideas. This makes them more creative in their works and decisions.

Emotional positivity enhances one's resilience to negative emotions. One develops more constructive, flexible coping, more abstract and long-term thinking and realizes a more emotional advantage or coverage following stressful or negative events. These are some of the qualities that any person and leader will want to harness in order to point to the team to their strengths and what they can achieve with their resources.

Emotional positivity can be learned through relaxation techniques like meditation, yoga, and muscle relaxation exercises. Relaxation techniques bring contentment, the very first feeling that reverses and resists negative emotions and their effects. The other way is to find positive meanings in events. This can be done by reframing adverse events in a positive light, or instilling ordinary events with positive values, or pursuing and attaining realistic goals.

Finding positive meaning requires you to be mindful of it and you will find it in situations. This will reward you with flowing experience of a whole range of positive emotions even in the worst circumstances. Smile and keep smiling.

Be it fake or real. Your brain reacts to your smile by releasing 'chemicals of happiness' that impact positively on your mind.

Whatever your occupation in life, find something you love and do it as regularly as possible. Do you sing, play soccer, or love cooking or reading? Create time for and work at it as often as is possible. It will help you to relax, feel good and forget about the outside world for a moment. Have your favorites at hand and make them a part of your schedules.

Positive emotions are good feelings that indicate that you are flourishing as a human being. Some of the positive feelings include joy, gratitude, serenity, hope, pride, amusement, inspiration, awe, and love. These feelings are not only desirable for you as a leader, but being contagious, they are very beneficial to the team as well. Let's look at some values that go with a positive attitude.

Gratitude

It is important to develop the quality of being thankful as a leader. Many a leader strive to show confidence, strength, honesty, passion, and persuasiveness. Only a few consciously nurture and cultivate gratitude as one of their values. Many think of it as a sign of weakness. Conversely, gratitude is described as a human strength by major religions. It not only promotes personal enhancement but also connects with your overall well-being and accomplishment of your goals.

Good leaders find gratitude to be the parent of all virtue. Beyond being a behavior of the one who expresses it, elicits a response from one receiving it. It propels helping behavior and increases support to, even, strangers. Gratitude builds relationships. That is, it produces emotional and interpersonal benefits.

Gratitude can be viewed as a scale for morals and motives and expressing it equates to discovering moral behavior and its enactment. You express gratitude in virtues. Rather than think of it as just an emotion, you need to perceive it as the embodiment of your entire approach to life being clear with intentions and deep internal change. It sets you up for more success.

As a leader, you will find it rewarding to show gratitude to your team. People know that gratitude is a virtue that is not common to all. When you exemplify gratitude, you gain the respect of others because they regard you among the few virtuous personalities. This respect exhibits in many positive behaviors that are beneficial for the team and its objectives.

Gratitude cannot be faked. It is not possible to consistently and congruently show gratitude when you do not mean it. People test you and know that you are sincere with your sentiments and actions of gratitude. When they make certain that you always mean it, they develop trust in you. To gain the trust of your team means you have their back to navigate through change or challenging situations.

We appreciate virtue when we see it in others. And a leader who shows the virtue of gratitude receives appreciation from the team that they lead. Gratitude effectively exalts positive emotions. People who give and receive gratitude rarely get angry. The often-angry persons are rarely grateful. Emotions of anger and jealousy can be neutralized by a simple sentiment or act of gratitude. When you are drawn toward being a grateful leader to your team, you will not find reason to micromanage or be authoritarian or rude to them.

Showing gratitude must be done with intentionality. You must have the ultimate objective of being grateful to a person. You do not need to give gratitude in a vacuum or for the sake of it. Gratitude is naturally objective, so you should be, too, when you exercise it. It is also important to only show genuine gratitude. You cannot fake it for so long. Practice it to cultivate it with intentionality.

Try to be frequent in showing gratitude. Do not wait for a reminder or major accomplishment. There are so many often smaller things and deeds you can be grateful for daily. The more you think about it, the more you will find the opportunity to be grateful. Be sure, however, not to overdo it or become petty in the practice of doing it. Be specific with what causes you to be grateful to someone. Mention what they did and how it served you or someone else.

Counting Your Blessings

In a world where everybody wants to have everything and be everywhere, by now many are left to focus on the gap between their more successful counterparts and them. Whatever they do, they do it in an attempt to make up. It is easy to lose one's own track for others' when one constantly thinks of themselves as disadvantaged and unprogressive. The spirit of competition makes many people falsely see more of other people's successes than their own.

Count your blessings, not your troubles. Recognize that you have resources to do what you want with and take you where you need. Having a future goal is good. However, create every chance to appreciate how far you have already come, and all you have accomplished. It is about the steps you have made, not what you want to do. You have something to build on. This is supposed the ideal mentality even when you are in the middle of tough times. Always focus on the positives.

It is what you feel inside that will drive you to do things on the outside. If you feel the right emotions in the inside, you will enact the right decisions and actions on the outside. Your emotional well-being is directly reflected in your beliefs, actions, and eventual results thereof. This is important for you as a leader because your beliefs and actions are reflected in the way the individuals carry themselves. What could have been only yours is manifested in the whole team, and its effect multiplied over.

As a leader, controlling your state in a positive way is critical for the success of the team. Great leaders know that focusing on troubles is distracting and detractive at the same time. It wastes time and resources. It destroys initiative, imagination, and action. Better to find something positive to be grateful for than to dwell on the negative aspects of your challenges.

Feeling blessed makes you come across as attractive all the time, even in the midst of tragedy. People respect you, listen to you, and choose to follow you on that basis. If you want to lead your team into success, you need their support and trust. How guaranteed you are of this when they think of you as blessed. But you will also need to demonstrate that you believe in who they are and what they can offer. Make your blessedness be contagious to them.

Making a Daily Choice to be Happy

How do you see yourself as a leader? How do you consider the past? And what do you see for the future? As a leader, you are required to break from, and cease to be, a prisoner of that sad, old past and instead become a pioneer of the happier, brighter future ahead. A dynamic growing sense of leadership always hopes to handle things better the next time around. It says, 'I can take more responsibility for how I respond to circumstances and people.' This is the daily mindset of a progressive leadership mind.

To be happy, you must choose to become responsible for yourself. Come to the realization that you must exit the victim-mentality and exit the victim-mode and choose how you feel by reworking your pattern of thinking and behavior. Develop the determination to make situations better for yourself and others. Establish what you have to do by yourself and where you will need the help of others, and be prompt in calling things to put through action. Know your thoughts and choose which ones to focus on for the sake of happiness and activity.

Realize that you have resources that suffice to undertake your course and responsibilities. Stop any comparisons. The inside of you is incomparable. And that is where the real job happens. Do not focus on the outside of others' lives and wish that for your own inside. People have their strengths and weaknesses. They have their successes and failures. That is their story, and it is different from yours. As for you, you need to know your doubts and limitations and appreciate them. Find solace in the thought that no one isn't lacking in their own way. Set yourself apart in a distinctive way, and be happy that way.

Accept yourself. Practice this daily. No one will do it for you. What are your endowments? How differently are you abled? What do you make of these toward the advancement of your livelihood? What advantages do they present in your life goals? How are you daily riding on your faculties to strengthen them and better your life? Recognize that everyone has their struggles. No one lacks one. But practicing daily self-acceptance and having compassion for yourself and your journey makes a major difference for you.

Live as your true self. Just show up as you really are. Consider your values and purpose in life. Put your targets and strategies in a clear perspective. What are your favorites and dislikes? What do you consider to give in your moments of strength? And what do you take when you are at your weakest? How much do you compromise under varied circumstances?

Be true to yourself, and allow yourself to be vulnerable. This is who you are as a person, and you cannot be sorry for being you. Discover these details of your internal self, and shut out external messages that are inconsistent with your genuine being. Be honest with everyone, share your authentic persona, and work with the world.

It is also important to create your daily routines of happiness. It is not rational to expect to be happy when you achieve milestones or possessions without first enjoying the journey along the way. You do not expect to constantly endure a course of unhappiness without giving up or going wrong. Set daily, regular commitments to yourself and your loved ones, and be sensitive when you accomplish them. That is what matters. It positions you to follow happiness much quicker. Be happy and make a happy team.

The Law of Positive Attraction

The people you attract in your life, the ideas that hatch in your mind, and the resources that come your way, are all a result of, and in harmony with, your dominant thoughts. The kinds of people you draw into your team are a reflection of what goes on in your thoughts most of the time. And they will bring ideas that are either not divergent from or consistent with or supportive of your own. It may be nature or destiny's way of bringing people together, but it has more about and to do with you.

When you grow and mature your leadership skills, you attract and retain better team membership. The dissonant personalities are repelled, similarly with such ideas and unhelpful resources. However, the caliber of people you deserve is dependent on your level of personal and professional development. This is determined by the kind of ideas you exchange and their relevance in your goals and targets.

The more you learn and grow, the more experiences you get to benefit from. The wiser you become, the faster and more consistent you grow. Invest in yourself. When you get better, your life gets better. The better manager you become, the better your people become. Your customers become better when you become a better salesperson. Your business becomes better when you become a better businessperson.

As a leader, you must keep improving yourself in order to improve all aspects of your life. Take charge, because you are in control. Read about the best practices and skills of leadership to apply in your field and personal development. Listen to audio lessons on strategies for successful leadership. Attend seminars and idea exchange hubs so you can gain new perspectives to help improve your operations.

Channeling Energy and Enthusiasm to Motivate

As a leader, you play a critical role to keep your team motivated on a daily basis. In fact, the effective energy that is required at work is not to be sourced from sleep, nutrition, and exercise, but from interactions at the workplace. Working at motivating your team will make them work harder and stay focused on tasks. More self-drive and greater enjoyment for work among your team lead to increased performance.

Always show a positive attitude. This is critical for your leadership to be effective. Show support, grace, and optimism in every activity, in every way possible. Be creative at it. Show appreciation at how the people are exerting their energies toward meeting targets. Where you feel you disagree on certain ideas, show respect for their opinion and seek common ground rather than shoot it down. Problems and crises shall arise. But you will need to focus on what you can and have to do rather than complain about what you cannot. A positive attitude is contagious, and the results of this effect cannot be more desired.

Relate with your group at a human level. Leadership is not just about assigning tasks and asking for results. Aim to cultivate and harness a two-way relationship with every individual of your team. Develop genuine interest in their emotions, concerns, happiness, and how they communicate. Show some vulnerability. Admit your mistakes, for instance, and commit to correct them in a timely manner. Show honesty and accountability, and be realistic in your actions; they will emulate the same from you.

Share your passion with your team. This brings them from the unending feeling of being in the dark in their lines of duty and sheds light on what they do. It rejuvenates their souls of work. Let them understand what connects you to your work so they can be influenced meaningfully. Share your goals, forthcoming projects, and missions. Let them know why you do everything you do, and you will be amazed by how excited and involved they will be at work.

Create an intellectually stimulating environment for the people to learn, challenge, and grow their faculties. Share your knowledge, lessons, and experiences. Listen to how they reason on issues and learn from them too. Receive their feedback, and give yours both at group and individual levels. Maintain an environment in which open dialogue, creativity, and question assumptions are encouraged. You will reap higher quality solutions that factor individual perspectives. Frequent open conversations between workers are opportunities for them to learn from each other and enhance their personalities and resources.

Developing Empathy

It is desirable that you should lead from the front and go way ahead to gather detail for progress. However, you are also required to sometimes get out of your own shoes and take a walk in their shoes so you can know what is happening around them. Expressing empathy creates bonds of trust with individuals. It gives insight into people's thoughts and feelings, and helps you better understand how they react. This should then help you sharpen your perception and intuition, and inform the kind of decisions you make for them.

Be a good listener and truly listen to everyone when you have the chance. Listen and be receptive to your eyes, ears, and heart. Observe the body language, tonal voice, and the hidden emotions behind the statements. Exercise patience in your listening. Do not keep thinking about what you are going to say next. Do not cut them off or rush them to finish their narration. Do not also jump to suggestions and judgments, but let them say what they have while you show your understanding. Being a good leader takes a personal interest in your members' well-being, and they will be more responsive and enduring to duty.

Empathy in the Workplace

Research findings suggest that people are less empathetic nowadays than a few decades before. And empathy remains undervalued at the workplace. But when exercised, it has a good impact on business performance as workers are motivated and their productivity is increased.

The tasks make our brains keep running and running. It is good to find time stop and reorient ourselves to our surroundings at the workplace. When our brains are too busy and loud, we even cease to sense our feelings, let alone others'. It tends to cause us to lose touch with life outside the office – family, friends, fun, personal initiative, etc. It is important to find time to breathe, take a walk, and clear the mind daily during break hours and evaluate what you are really thinking and feeling.

Be sensitive to your feelings; then, you can understand the others'. Create an emotion inventory of what events trigger what feelings in you at the workplace. Try to apply your findings to others. You will find your matches in a number of scenarios. Notice any changes in your workmates, and try to find out how they are doing.

Be sensitive to your communications (e.g. always begin by salutation in your email conversations). Sometimes, use a telephone to hear how they speak on the phone. Better yet, video conferencing can allow you to see how colleagues are feeling if you cannot reach them physically. The communication technology at the workplace matters in this respect.

Laying support systems for employees help to actualize what empathy can mean at the workplace. Encourage workers to join welfare organizations or launch one right there. Establish motivational and reward systems, and put them to good use.

It is important to show empathy in the right circumstances, in the right manner, and for the right reasons. Empathy helps a team to work more cohesively, which is good for business.

Emotional Intelligence Test

Emotional intelligence is important for every person and leader. As a leader, you must be able to read, regulate, and harness your emotions beneficially, as well as observe other people's and respectively help them accordingly.

You need to evaluate your emotions by looking at your personal traits and your capability to handle or cope with the traits. Personal traits include how fast you get excited, underwhelmed, bored, angered, upset, confused, etc. You then need to evaluate what these emotions cause you to do. Are you tempted to lie, overcommit, shout, withdraw, attack, etc? Finally, what do you do to stop these emotions and their likely effects?

Consider yourself in the light of the following with short answers:

    i.   How often and deeply or widely do you experience negative emotions?

    ii.   Can you manage stressful situations maintaining your cool?

    iii.   How assertive are you when in difficult emotions?

    iv.   Are you a proactive or reactive person in the presence of a difficult person?

    v.   How quickly do you bounce back from adversity?

vi. Do you frequently and freely express intimate emotions in your close and personal relationships?

Describe yourself with adequate detail and in an adequate manner using precise terminologies under the following situation:

i. How often do you come under stressful or frustrating situations and how do you handle them?

ii. How do you regard and handle failures and discouragements?

iii. What are your leadership skills and methods for achieving success?

iv. What methods do you use to manage the emotions of others of different ages?

v. What methods do you use to assess various personality traits in other people?

vi. How do you deal with diversity and cultural sensitivities?

Chapter 5:

Interpersonal Skills and Emotionally Intelligent Communication

Interpersonal skills refer to one's ability to communicate and interact well with others. It also comprises the ability to control one's own emotions and manage them. Having interpersonal skills is quite foundational in anyone's success. People who are full of personal skills seem to work with others better than those without. They also communicate more effectively, and are able to establish and maintain better relationships at both the workplace and home.

Developing interpersonal skills requires one to become aware of how they interact with other people and consciously begin to practice these skills in their interactions. Interpersonal skills include communication skills, emotional intelligence, teamwork, leadership, flexibility, responsibility, dependability, motivation, negotiation, persuasion and influencing skills, patience, empathy, conflict resolution and mediation, and problem-solving and decision making.

Wherever you lead your life, you do not live in a bubble. You live and meet with people with whom you interact and communicate daily. Interpersonal skills help in your interactions to make it easier and more pleasant for you and those you interact with. In the long run, you end up building better and lasting relationships both at home and at work.

Interpersonal skills will help you to communicate better with family and friends and solve issues more easily and quickly before they escalate into bigger problems. At the workplace is where you spent most of your day with your colleagues or teammates, suppliers, customers, and clients. You must learn to leverage interpersonal skills in order to be more productive, and advance your business objectives, lest you later begin to wonder what went wrong. The importance of interpersonal skills cannot be overemphasized.

Emotional intelligence regards one's ability to listen well, motivate and inspire others, control one's reactions, and build strong relationships. It helps one to react to situations consciously and consistently in a measurable manner. An emotionally intelligent person is able to filter their responses verbally and tonally and display appropriate congruent body language to emphasize the communications. This helps them enhance their relationships with employers, business partners, investors, and their friends and family.

While it can come naturally in a number of people, emotional intelligence can be attained through learning and practicing. One keeps at it until they can recognize, control, and leverage on their emotions to be more effective with their business and personal communications. Being emotionally intelligent will help you to be heard more accurately, inspire, and motivate as well as amplify your overall leadership manifestation.

Just because you feel emotions doesn't mean you have to act on them. But at the same time, emotional intelligence should not prevent you from manifesting your emotions when it is necessary. Rather, you will often consider separating yourself from causative situations for a while to gain your composure. That way, you come to a position to evaluate how best to relay your emotions for efficiency and effectiveness of communication.

Developing Interpersonal Skills

Interpersonal skills are a fundamental component for your good-working, your social relationships, and for developing your other areas of skill. You need confidence, empathy, and communication skills in order to realize the most out of every interaction. Interpersonal skills are not only this important, but they will also help you make more friends and demonstrate your capability to highlight the strengths of others at the workplace.

A smart businessperson is a smart communicator too. They know how to interact with people and handle issues by interacting. They can use every possible thing to build scope and resources. The interpersonally skilled also know how to use individuality and groups, and is way ahead in their professional and personal lives.

i. Cultivate a Positive Outlook

Teach yourself to be positive. Keep in mind the benefits of your life and job. Learn to show maturity in your thoughts and talks. Whenever you set out to embark at your work and you feel upset, try to suppress your negative feelings until after work. Stressful work issues arise from time to time, but even in them, you have to find positive aspects and build on them to come out more optimistic.

Keeping a positive outlook is not only showing respect to yourself, but also honoring the business you run and the job you do. Be cheerful, smiling, and open in your interactions with your teammates, colleagues, customers, suppliers, and clients. You will get more out of them in return.

ii. Control Your Emotions

There is not necessarily a place to be overly emotional if you would like to communicate or work effectively. When you feel extremely irritated, severely depressed, or ecstatically happy, breathe deeply in and tone your emotions down. However the situation looks, always focus on what outcome you want out of it, and consider what you want to address in your communication in relation to that outcome. Express yourself in a calm and patient manner.

iii. Cooperate with and Appreciate Others

Reach out to your colleagues for their support and to support them. Do not work alone. Inquire for their views, ideas, and inputs, and listen to what they offer. Remember to give back when approached in the same vein. Let them know you appreciate their expertise, and that you are ready to offer yours too when needed. Ask for their help and give credit where due, and you will promote harmony and trust be it at home or at the workplace.

iv. Demonstrate Real Interest in Others

You spend time with people doing work at the office, or attending to your business, or just promoting your social welfare at home or in groups. It is only fair that you get to know them better. Learn something about their lives, what they consider important, their concerns and worries, their opinions on issues, and their interests in life and career. It will help to solidify your relations with them.

v. Look Out for Others' Strengths

People differ because we are all unique individuals. You will regularly have to interact with people whose personality is a direct opposite of yours. However, you should not let personal differences get in the way of peak performance. Business has to run. Tasks need to be accomplished. Targets must be met. Look out for one good professional trait in them, and cooperate on that value to benefit everyone and the business.

vi. Practice Active Listening

Create time to listen to your teammates or colleagues and even family. Listening is a way of telling people you care about them. Active listening means giving them more time to speak while you listen patiently with interest. Make eye contact, nod, lean in toward them, and repeat what they say to affirm your present senses and mind during conversation. Make the speaker feel respected as you listen. Try to show that you take action on or remember what you have discussed previously.

vii. Take Responsibilities

Train yourself to take responsibility and accountability for your thoughts and actions. Show some vulnerability and accept correction where necessary. Accept your mistakes and learn from them, beyond seeking assistance or fixing them yourself. This will help reduce tension and conflict with other people. Ultimately, you will become more efficient and productive, and earn the respect and love of others.

Listening Skills

Genuine listening is like gifting someone your time. It falls among the first steps for building relationships, solving problems, ensuring understanding, resolving conflicts, and even improving accuracy. Effective listening at the workplace results in minimal errors and maximum leverage on time. When children develop the skill of listening at home, they become self-reliant and able to solve their problems from an early age. Listening enhances friendships and careers as well as saves money and marriages. Let us take a look at a few skills necessary for listening.

i.   Face the Speaker

Naturally, the desire to communicate people pulls them together from the other room. When close enough, it is important to face the speaker with your whole body -the face, body, and feet all the same. Maintain eye contact and avoid any eye distractions. If the speaker does not face you, excuse them for their reasons but stay focused yourself.

ii.   Remain Attentive and Relaxed

Do not stare fixedly. Look away frequently, but remain attentive with your whole. Avoid any mental distractions, like background noises. Forgive the speaker's accent and speech mannerisms. Also, do not be carried away in your own thoughts, feelings, and biases.

iii. Stay Open-Minded

Do not judge or criticize what is said in your mind. You may look alarmed when you are, but do not make unfavorable comments or jump to conclusions. Listen to every thought and feeling as they come from their minds. Do not grab sentences and finish on their stead. Get their train of thoughts to completion.

iv. Create Mental Pictures

Allow your mind to envision models of what is being communicated. Stay focused with all of your senses; be alert. Do not start thinking about what you want to say next. Concentrate. Force your mind to refocus when tempted to wander mentally.

v. Be Patient

Treat the speaker as being important, and show you care what they are thinking. Slow down to their pace of conversation, and do not suggest solutions unless asked. Wait for longer pauses to ask questions.

vi. Do Not Distract

Do not interrupt when someone is addressing you. Also, do not distract with the questions you ask. Be careful to let the speaker tell their story to the end without redirecting it your way.

vii. **Show Empathy**

Feel with the speaker what they feel and convey that to them. Empathy is the heart and soul of good listening. Take their place in the situations and show you understand what it felt like without making further suggestions.

viii. **Give Regular Feedback**

Show you understand the message. Respond in a timely manner, and reflect feelings back to the speaker. Let them know you are listening and following their thoughts. Restate some statements to show or seek clarity of understanding.

ix. **Pay Attention to Non-Verbal Cues**

Pay attention to the body language, tonal voice, gestures and cues, facial expressions, and feelings behind words. There is a lot of detail that is being transmitted non-verbally. Do not ignore it.

How to Deal with Tension and Conflict More Constructively

Conflict is a natural part of life. We all have differing opinions over some matter. Not that some are better than or superior over the others, but that our beliefs, experiences, and values distinguish us from each other. We desire to address conflicts in such a way that we come out better and enhance a common purposefulness in the many different ways that we do.

i. Define the Conflict and Focus on It

Sit together and frame out the conflict in every possible detail with clarity and precision. Know exactly the who, what, when, where and why. Describe the behaviors and feelings and their consequences and desired changes. The descriptions must bear the views from all involved parties. Do not focus on the people.

ii. Brainstorm the Solutions

Take turns to offer your solution alternatives and write them down. Do not judge each other's ideas yet. Be patient and trust the process.

iii. Analyze Each of Them

For each of the suggested solutions, examine their strengths and weaknesses. Think and talk positively, and shun all negativity. Listen carefully. Identify your points of convergence and divergence.

iv. Agree on The Most Workable Solution

Agree on the most viable and practical solution that is understandable and bearable to both of you. Develop a plan to expedite your resolution steps.

v. Apply the Solution

Commit and follow through your plan to resolve the conflict. Attend to every detail of action agreed upon.

vi. Keep Evaluating

Work out a way to see how well the solution is working, and make adjustments where necessary. Keep building on the successes until final victory is achieved.

Remember to treat each other with respect throughout the resolution process and communicate understanding throughout it.

Conflict Management Techniques

i. Accommodating

This method is also called Smoothing. You consider giving your opponent their wishes and ignore your own. This is when you consider the issue petty to you, so you want to keep the peace, accept you are wrong, or buy time until you have resources to resolve the issue later. It will allow you time to reassess the situation and protect more important things.

ii. Avoiding

You sidestep, postpone, or withdraw, and hope that the conflict will resolve itself without confrontation. This you choose when you feel weaker or inferior, when you see the issue as trivial, when there is evident hostility in the process, or when the process is too draining emotionally, financially, etc. Like when you accommodate, avoiding will allow you time to reassess the situation and protect more important things.

iii. Collaborating

You integrate ideas from all conflicting parties and make a creative win-win solution acceptable to everyone. It can be time-consuming. It is useful when consensus and contribution of others are necessary, when there is a high level of trust or long-term relationship that is more important, or when responsibility is to be shared. Beyond solving the problem, this method reinforces the trust and respect between the parties.

iv. Compromising

The affected parts give up some elements of their stances to reach an agreeable or acceptable solution. This occurs when the parties hold averagely equivalent power, when a temporary solution is first desired before complex details are addressed, or when the parties are new to each other. It can be a faster way to lower tension and stress following the conflict.

v. Competing

This is when one party pursues its concerns despite resistance from the other. It works when you have to stand up for your rights and resist aggression or pressure, and all other resolution strategies have failed. It can be quick or even give a solution to long-standing conflicts. It can also reward with increased self-esteem and respect if one was standing up to resist aggression and hostility.

Learn How to Give Honest and Candid Feedback Appropriately

Very few people look forward to feedback occasions with joy and pleasure. But everyone wants to get honest feedback nonetheless. Giving feedback is critical, but difficult too. We do not want to hurt others, but we also do not want to live in resentment with them. But feedback conveyed in a supportive manner fosters motivation, improvement, resilience, and psychological safety where issues are addressed in an open manner. So, do you relay feedback?

i. Focus More on The Positive Than Negative

Give at least three supportive, appreciative, and encouraging observations for every one critical, disapproving, and contradictory one. Bad is stronger than good because our brains dwell more on negative feedback. To engage more with your colleagues, communicate positively. You are free to correct, criticize, and confront, and as long as you do it in a positive context, you will get positive results out of it.

ii. Comment on The Strengths

Do not focus on the critical bits. Bring out their unique contributions and best self-demonstrations. The person will be encouraged to strive for excellence in their competencies. Be specific on the strong points as on the negative ones and give examples and details to the feedback. Overcome the tendency to be partial with the positive and exaggerative with the negative feedback.

iii. Emphasize Collaboration and Team Spirit

Remain objective when you speak about negative events. Describe them rather than evaluate them. Rather than place blame, identify associated objective consequences or personal feelings. Then go on to suggest viable alternatives without arguing who is right or at fault.

Learn How to Receive Negative Feedback Constructively

Feedback in whatever form can have a positive impact. It helps assess whether one is doing the right thing or can improve. Criticism, implemented constructively, can increase performance, productivity, and effectiveness. Rather than getting angry and defensive, consider the following helpful suggestions.

i. Reflect in Silence

See if the opinion is backed with facts about you or is inaccurately derived. If you find evidence in your mind, then calmly communicate back and take it constructively. Plan to act on it with timelines, and finally communicate the resolution when done.

ii. Take it Objectively

Do not take it personally. It is not a mature way, either. Actions do not necessarily reflect on you. Use it to better change and improve yourself.

iii. Think Present and Future

Rather than recap how it could have been prevented or done better, try to address the issue in the moment. Find the solution and apply it, and then reflect to improve the process going forward.

iv. Consider the Critic

Negative feedback can be fine to try handling but not destructive feedback. The source must have similar goals as yours; be aware of the situational context and present a new perspective. If such elements are inconsistent, then it is not worth consideration.

v. Reframe and Ask for Clarification

Think that all feedback is useful. If you sense a new dimension, then it provides a chance for improvement. If you think it is undeserved, then ask for clarification as to how they arrived at the opinion.

vi. Prioritize to Preserve Communications

If you regard the source in a way, then let them know you heard just to keep the communication lines open. Or, thank them and ask a follow-up question so you get conversing about their complaint. Later, you can filter what is of use for improvement.

Good Interpersonal Behaviors

Strong interpersonal skills can be indicative of success in any environment as individuals cooperate, get to solve problems, and know and appreciate each other better and better. Beyond your qualification credits, you need to able to fit in the company culture and contribute to its growth.

i. Emotional Intelligence

Always keep your emotions in check so that you can navigate social situations with composure. Strive to keep your calm even under pressure and contain your frustrations. Always face situations with objectivity, being mindful of others' feelings.

ii. Communication

Learn to articulate ideas to others with clarity and precision. Be a team player. Train yourself with body language, non-verbal cues, and gestures so that your communications are clear from the inside and outside.

iii. Reliability

Develop a good work ethic and have the integrity to get things done. Always keep time, fulfill your promises, and give high quality. You want respect and reputation, and that is how you earn them.

iv. Leadership

Stay motivated and inspired, and take charge when tasks need to be accomplished. Create operational plans, and help people give their best in deserving situations. Exude self-confidence and vision, and be an example in all ways possible.

v. Positivity

This is the formula for success and popularity. Keep a cheerful attitude and show optimism in all your work. Be mindful of your morale and approach the tense moments with a calm, upbeat attitude.

vi. Negotiation

Learn to engage in and take charge of discussions for finding shared agreement. Be a quick and critical thinker, and be creative at solving problems in such a way that all the parties feel satisfied.

vii. Teamwork

Rely on and support each other in every simple and hard task. Know when to show leadership and when to stand back. Share feedback and help each other to become their best in their personal and professional lives.

viii. Listening

Be willing to listen to and respect others. Be open to their ideas. Seek clarity and demonstrate your interest in their concerns. Practice active listening. Reach out for their social well-being, and get to understand them better. Show empathy, too, and handle the issue in a consistent manner with how they feel.

How to Work Well with People

The phrase 'Must be able to work well with people' is almost cliché in open job requirements. Many ignore it. But it is actually a warning that you could be fired on that premise. Promotions and career advancements can be based on quite simple things. Here is a list of some of them.

i.   Always put your phone away unless you are using it for official purposes

ii.   Assume the best of your colleagues and go for that in them

iii. Avoid interrupting work with noise or not-settling behaviors

iv. Share credit with the team even when you deserved it alone

v. Check your body language for charisma

vi. Respond to emails soonest and always

vii. Stay positive, optimistic, inspired, and smile for happiness and success

viii. Always be honest and tactful in your sentiments

ix. Practice active listening and empathy

x. Take responsibility

xi. Know when to say 'no'

xii. Be open-minded

xiii. Keep time

xiv. Remember people's names and know their individualities

xv. Show sincere appreciation

xvi. Keep improving yourself

Showing Appreciation

Everyone wants to be appreciated. It then follows, everyone needs to show appreciation. No specific occasion is necessary. In fact, the tiny gestures of appreciation shown throughout the year are valued more than an extreme gesture of appreciation shown once a year. The following are some ways that leaders can show appreciation to their workers:

i.   Give regular praise for a job well done

ii. Find time to say 'Thank You'

iii. Ask their interests outside of work

iv. Offer flexible scheduling

v.   Present personalized gifts

vi. Give financial incentives

vii. Treat them to a meal

viii. Create a fun culture

ix. Bring little surprises

x.   Provide an opportunity for growth and advancement

Chapter 6:

Change and Resistance Management with EI

1. Management of change

Adaptability is a skill that has to be learned and is central as part of one's emotional intelligence. In an organization, no one wants to be the person that lags behind. However, some people are resistant to change, and a leader has to be emotionally intelligent to deal with such issues. Therefore, some strategies can be used to reduce resistance so that everyone is ready to embrace change rather than brace for it.

i. Identify the source of resistance

There is always a reason that drives resistance. One needs to identify the reason for opposition. This requires one to have very high levels of self-awareness. For example, a person might resist change because it might make them look less competent. In this case, identification of the underlying reason can enable one to create a lifeline that will ensure they do not end up a failure. Alternatively, a person might be scared that change might impede their autonomy. Speaking out this concern will enable the leaders to involve them so that they are in charge of the decision-making process. Even if the change is not favorable to a person, involvement gives a person control, and that can help deal with the resistance.

ii.   Identify   the   basis   for   the response.

Emotional reactions are often a result of people's perceptions, and they have convinced themselves that they are correct. Therefore, they might not be in line with reality. However, since a person has convinced himself of a particular fact, they might resist the change, even if it is right for them.

It is pertinent for a person to identify the basis of an emotional response, and question the primary emotion associated with it. Once the primary feeling has been identified, it will be easier to be objective and probe what it is really about. The questioning process will help one identify the perception they have of reality, and the stories that drive their emotions. Thus, rational thought will thrive in the end, and the resistance will be dealt with.

An example is a technologist who was angry when recruits came into the company. She identified her intense emotional reaction as anger. When further probing was done, she understood that she felt powerless, and was scared she would become useless as recruits continued to come in. This realization made her be objective and separate her emotional reaction and perception from the actual events that were going on in the company. She was able to list several options for leadership and was able to take back her power. A shift in her thought process occurred, and she was able to stop thinking that power was being taken from her to thinking of ways she can leverage different leadership positions to her advantage.

iii.   Take ownership

Taking responsibility for a negative situation is not easy, and it is pertinent for a person to fess up and take ownership for their part in the case. Self-awareness is central here, and one is supposed to take note of how their attitudes and behavior led to the current situation. By being mindful of how a person's response leads to adverse events, it will be easier to break the cycle and be a beacon for change in an organization. It will also be easy to manage an attitude that led to pessimistic behavior, and be open to new ideas and perspectives.

Taking ownership also makes one aware of the influence they have on others and what they can do to drive an organization forward. People in positions of power have an immense impact on others, and their attitudes directly or indirectly affect other people. Therefore, it is crucial for one to identify their influence, how their behavior affects the organization, and if they are being objective on how to promote change.

iv.   Be positive

Change is hard, especially if one does not see its importance. However, research has indicated that having a positive attitude can lead to new opportunities. For instance, being positive about the shift from analog to digital can open up new opportunities that the digital world provides. A positive outlook also makes one more receptive to change.

Significant questions to ask when being positive are what the opportunities are and how they might be beneficial to someone. Identifying opportunities involves high levels of self-awareness and motivation. One has to research and identify the way these opportunities might be right for them.

One has also to know that the ability to adapt to change is a competitive advantage, especially for leaders. Thus, a leader should be able to motivate his team to quickly adapt to change so that they can be better and be the leading team. Therefore, anytime one feels like they are resisting, they should remember that change puts them at an advantage, and they should get the energy to adapt to it and push it forward.

v.   Communication

The critical element that drives successful change in an organization is the leader's ability to communicate the need for change within the organization. Maintaining the status quo is comfortable, and many people in the organization will easily opt to preserve things the way they are. Specifically, it will be hard to enact change if people feel like the difference is of no importance to them, or it will waste their time. This is especially true for the older generation who see no need to learn new tricks.

The ability to effectively communicate the status quo about the change is instrumental in effecting change, and reducing resistance. Communication skills of the leader will be able to create dissatisfaction amongst the staff in situations where everyone is content with the way things are. Thus, a leader will create the urgency for change in members. It needs a leader who is highly self-aware, motivated and is aware of the abilities of everyone in the organization. The initial communication process must generate anxiety and fear, and all the emotions of the people who are to change.

vi.   Implement teamwork.

Leaders who try to enact change alone are less likely to succeed. Involving others in the change process is pertinent in promoting change and lowering resistance levels. Therefore, a leader should be smart and put together a winning team, that will easily influence others to accept the change.

The coalition chosen should be enthusiastic, smart, and very good communicators. The goal of communication is to pass the message fast and push for the implementation of critical decisions. Leaders should actively appeal to the ethos, logos, and pathos of members to motivate them to achieve excellence under the new system.

Emotionally intelligent leaders should identify the motivating factors and act on them so that excellence is achieved. For some people, motivation is in the money, and for some, it is job satisfaction. Therefore, a leader should provide the tools necessary, according to the motives of members, and then actively push for change. This will reduce resistance because members will not see the role as a chore, but as a passion that fulfills their desires.

The chosen team should be assigned to different people, so that management of the change process is more natural. The localization of power will also make it easier for motivating factors to be identified and acted on accordingly.

vii.   **Work on social skills**.

Empathetic people understand when to use emotions and when to use the voice of reason when appealing for change. Therefore, good leaders and team members are highly self-aware, can self-regulate easily, and are very empathetic. These social skills should be used in building and maintaining friendships and other relations.

Trust is central in the formation of change, irrespective of how the team was formed. Therefore, it should be emphasized in every step of the change. A person has to be trustworthy, have integrity, and be open to change. Leaders should be able to think before they act to build trust, be able to keep their work and be ready to learn from anyone.

To promote change, one can use emotions, to appeal to the people's emotional state. If a person can relate to the idea at an emotional level, they can personalize the process, and be receptive to it. Thus, resistance levels will go low. Alternatively, one can use reason and tell the people why the change is essential and urgent. Proper communication of the ideas, backed by evidence, will appeal to the logos of the people involved, and they will be more receptive to the change.

2. How to overcome resistance

There are two types of strength in an organization-rational and irrational resistance. Rational resistance is whereby there is no involvement from members, while irrational opposition involves opposition from members. People who resist rationally can be persuaded to accept the change. Therefore, emotionally intelligent leaders use social skills to push for change.

When such a leader encounters irrational resisters, emotional skills are used to persuade change. To start, the leader should identify the reasons for the resistance. It can be low self-esteem, incompetence, fear of the unknown, and fear of losing something.

i.)   Identify emotions

Change within any environment disrupts the emotional temperature of a place. Therefore, it can lead to demotivation or motivation, depending on the morale of the employees. An emotionally intelligent leader identifies his emotions, and those of employees, and manages these emotions well, as well as the people. Bad feelings should be controlled or redirected to positive energy which can be channeled to enhance change.

Highly self-aware leaders are confident in their abilities, and employees want a leader who believes in himself. Therefore, if followers see that leaders are confident in the change that they are pushing for, the same confidence will be affected by the followers. Implementation of such a project will be easy.

ii.)   Have patience

Research has indicated that some leaders lack the patience to get things done in a company. There is a sense of urgency that drives leaders to get things done immediately. Change is an aspect that takes time, and the lack of patience can lead to resistance. Followers must be involved through the whole process so that the vision for the change is realized, as the change is enacted.

Leaders have to create a community where the needs and wants of everyone involved are included in the process. Thus, a system whereby everyone has shared values and is moving towards the same vision will be created, and resistance levels will go low. This process requires a lot of patients from the leaders.

iii.) Empathy

It is an essential skill that can be used to reduce resistance. Leaders should listen and understand the follower's point of view. They should be able to identify the concerns of other people and use their social skills to persuade those who are not ready to change. On the same note, the diverse needs of the population have to be addressed, because a large part of the modern workforce is different. Therefore, understanding the concerns of everyone is essential when pushing for change to reduce resistance. Moreover, such leaders know that the reaction a person has to change is an indication of underlying fears, and does everything possible to do away with this fear.

Followers should also be empathetic to each other so that the concerns of others are addressed. Some people might be ready to change and have the urgency to change. However, a team is only as strong as its weakest member. Therefore, each teammate should be prepared to accommodate the other and reduce resistance amongst the members.

iv.)   Self-awareness

It is the foundation for emotional intelligence because a person is only able to understand and support others if he understands his weaknesses, strengths, and can manage their emotions well. A study done in American schools indicates that leaders who can easily manage their feelings can push for change and reduce resistance levels.

The levels by which followers accept change is dependent on the relationship leaders establish with all the members. Therefore, a highly self-aware leader can create a good relationship with all interest groups and use his social skills to reduce resistance. A well-liked leader is less likely to receive resistance, compared to a leader with poor social skills.

v.)   Ask for clarification

Resistance to change might be because the message is not clear. This mostly happens in organizations where the mode of communication is top-down. When information is not clear, people form their own stories and concoct their own realities. Thus, the consequences of the change in people's minds will be different from the truth. Therefore, it is paramount that clarification is sought so that everyone is on the same page.

Asking for clarification can be used by the leader to convince those who are resistant to the change. This is the time the leader will identify motivating factors, and convince everyone why the change is urgent and vital to them. Clarification can also be seeking to understand the objections the followers have. Some of the complaints might be realistic and have to be handled before the change is enacted.

vi.)   Use mediators if possible.

At times, a consensus between the leaders and followers can fail to be reached. A leader can try as much as he wants to persuade change, but the irrational resistance will take root, and prevent the switch from taking place. A mediator is a good idea when such a thing occurs. An emotionally intelligent leader understands that familiarity can cause people not to take a leader seriously. Therefore, a person with a different point of view can be useful to push for change.

The mediator will provide a fresh perspective and give other examples of how the change proposed has been successful. The mediator will also stand in the place of the leader, and concerns that could not be aired to the leader will be discussed. At the end of the meeting, all issues will be tabled, and clarity will be achieved.

A mediator will also take care of any disagreements, and arbitrate on behalf of the organization. Therefore, people who have irrational resistance will have no ground to stand on and resists the change. A fresh perspective is good, and it will make followers and leaders come to the same table with new rules and guidelines in place.

vii.) Be keen on body language

One should be able to accurately read a room, and discern what people are thinking. This is an essential strategy, that will help someone know how and when to communicate with people, especially when enacting change. One should be able to know when to appeal to emotions, and when to use logic.

The ability to read body language is also essential when identifying the motivating factors of followers. A leader can know when to push a subject and how to promote it. Some people's mode of communication is through actions, while some people need to be talked to. Therefore, a leader should be able to read a room and use his social skills to reduce resistance.

Chapter 7:

Mindfulness as an Emotionally Intelligent Leadership Practice

Mindfulness and Emotionally Intelligent

One cannot be emotionally intelligent without mindfulness of their emotions. We can only cultivate our emotional intelligence through being mindfully existent. Mindfulness is a key tool that helps us understand ourselves, our thoughts and feelings, and what is important to us. It develops our self-awareness, the foundational component on which emotional intelligence and its other associated skills spring from.

As a leader, you want to be more thoughtful and deliberate in your interactions with people. You want to be more present and alive understanding your emotional triggers, strengths and weaknesses, and motivations. These are exercised mindfully. Mindfulness is baseline consistency. If you want to connect to your happiness in life, then you must possess consistent emotional intelligence.

Let us review some facts about mindfulness:

i. Mindfulness enhances ability to understand own emotions

ii. Mindfulness develops the ability to detect and understand other people's emotions

iii. Mindfulness significantly enhances the ability to regulate and control own emotions

iv. Mindfulness allows and facilitates individuals to effectively use their emotions

v. Mindfulness fosters positive effects and inhibits negative ones yielding greater life satisfaction

vi. Mindfulness strengthen abilities to perceive, understand and regulate thoughts and emotions

vii. Mindfulness promotes attunement, connection, and closeness in relationships

viii. Mindfulness deepens insight into self, others and human nature eases ego-based concerns and encourages compassionate concern for others

ix. Mindfulness breeds empathy

x. Mindfulness enhances ability to uniquely connect with and serve individuals as unique human beings

xi. Mindfulness sharpens focus of mind to internal feelings

xii. Mindfulness improves attention, cognitive flexibility, and problem-solving capability

xiii. Mindfulness enhances composure during stressful situations

xiv. Mindfulness enhances one's state of preparedness

xv. Mindfulness improves mental capacity, speed, judgment, and creativity

Reading through the above facts, you might have realized that most of the facts are consistent with the various aspects and purposes of emotional intelligence. Essentially, mindful meditation empowers the mind to dominate judgment and decisions. While concern about self and others culminates in feelings and emotions, their justification cannot be founded except through reason and logic.

Emotional intelligence is the ability to identify and manage your emotions and those of others. You strive to use the emotions as resources, but not experience them as burdens. This takes mindful effort. Let us examine the three aspects of emotional intelligence:

i.   Emotional Awareness

Nurture and train your ability to perceive the emotions you feel and those around you feel. You notice the emotions without judging or altering them. You will learn how different people handle their emotions differently and come to appreciate your uniqueness, too. This will help you better accept who you are as a person and respect others in extension, which will lead to showing more love and compassion toward yourself and other humans.

ii.   Emotional Application

Develop your skill to utilize your emotions for the benefit of self and others. Your emotions should not clog, but help your thinking. For instance, you identify rumination, self-hate, and fear as negative thought patterns that result in stress and despair. Or rather than wallow in or dismiss negative feelings, acknowledge the associated negative emotions and master them by figuring out their sources.

iii.   Emotional Management

Focus on strengthening your ability to regulate your emotions. For instance, take time to reflect on your day-long feelings. As much possible, strive to stay positive, but recognize that negative emotions are also important sources of information. Lay an internal locus of control from where decisions are made, especially under stressful events.

There are some situations in which negative emotions are more reliable. Under such circumstances, it takes mindful techniques to approach tasks with the right frame of mind. Mindfulness creates a gap between stimulus and response creating an opportunity to direct creative responses that spur personal growth and freedom.

Mindfulness brings our subconscious to our conscious and forces emotions to lose grip so that we can respond intentionally and react reflexively. Mindfulness, in practice, fosters the ability to accurately sense and empathize with others' emotions and use awareness of our own and others to negotiate interactions skillfully. Mindfulness prepares you to recognize and observe the experience of distressing emotions, along with their negative thoughts with acceptance and perspective.

Mindfulness and Leadership

So how does mindfulness from the perspective of emotional intelligence influence leadership?

i.   Empathy

Empathy is the ability to understand what another feels while still being able to discern your own feelings. Understanding yourself better through practicing mindfulness helps you to understand other people's feelings, as well, and that way, you begin to empathize with them. You begin to pay attention to their body language, read their facial expressions and bodily cues, and get to know them better and how they are feeling.

Empathy goes further in developing connections between you and other people. You see their concerns and relate with your own with deeper understanding. Ultimately, empathy deepens relationships between the concerned people and makes their bonds grow stronger and stronger. This is a necessary trait and consequence that any good leader would desire to keep.

ii.   Difficult Conversation

Disagreements among people occur because of dissonance among them. As a leader, you will deal with many difficult conversations, and it will take this skill to work through conflicts in relationships. Mindfully, you will develop the capacity to understand your counterparts' perspective so that your judgment shall consider multidimensional views and not just yours.

Emotional conflicts heighten to conflicts when you stick to your own perspective; you want to avoid that. Rather, you go further, and even consider the impacts of your views on others. Are you getting angered or frustrated in the midst of the conversations? Take a pause. Hold on and do not react yet. Calm yourself down with a deep breath and, maybe, reflect for a moment.

Mindfully bring yourself back, be present in the conversation, and steer above the influence of emotions. When you are not overtaken by emotions, you make rational decisions and engage in a more productive conversation. Practice your mindfulness also to understand and empathize with the points of view of others so that you can create win-win solutions informed by both people's perspectives.

iii.   Compassion

Are you compassionate? When you have the willingness and capacity to be of service to those whose emotions you empathize with, then you have compassion. For instance, an employee gets emotionally triggered and begins to go into emotional ranting and you notice it. You step out to them and ask how you can offer support so they can begin to get out of the trigger. You still go ahead and discuss with them what caused the trigger and what you can do to avoid it in the future.

Similarly, try focusing on workers when they come into distress. If it is due to working on a certain task, then you give your support in it, assist them complete it and do mentorship on them. Help build their skills in that particular task for the future good. There are many instances in which you can exercise your leadership by showing compassion to your team individually or in groups.

The Benefits of Mindfulness and Emotional Intelligence

You, as a leader, stand to benefit in a number of ways from practicing mindfulness and exercising emotional intelligence in your roles.

i.   Trust

Emotional intelligence is worked at with mindfulness. To many, it is an acquired virtue that keeps growing stronger with use. You earn the trust of other people as a result of your patience to spend time, observing, listening, and communicating mindfully with them. People find you to be reliable and honest. These are complementary values that you acquire as a reward for giving yourself to meditation. The understanding you develop about the soul of humans enables you to understand people's emotions without judging them. This quality is noticed by the people and it endears you to them.

ii.   Resilience

Mindfulness trains focus on the mind and screening of what is essential from among the rubbles. The resilient remain steady in challenging situations and regard the emotions of theirs and others as sources of information that help to understand and overcome adversity. They are first to detect emotional distress in others as early symptoms of looming danger or signs of approaching successes.

They show the understanding of the emotional experiences of other people when assisting them. They do not impress their own ideologies on others because they appreciate the uniqueness of individuals. Their own experiences of the past give them the wisdom and strength to understand and serve others.

iii. Better Relationships

Mindful people are mindful of their relations and know the depths and widths of connections. They are patient to take time to build relationships. As much as possible, the mindful make their relations to depend on them more than their counterparts. They know how to impact strongly on their long-term relations through the briefest interactions they make with people around them.

Mindful leaders are always aware of their motivation and the reasons they keep choosing to lead. They distinguish between their needs and those of others and prioritize to serve others first. To them, service to self is first through service to others. They mind how they treat others as they go about meeting goals. They put people over projects.

They set clear expectations and communicate them effectively. They make sure expectations are reasonable and achievable. They assign tasks with an understanding of the knowledge, skills, and abilities of the team. They provide sufficient empowerment and support so the team to achieve their agreed-upon goals. And they monitor progress and address any situations before they arise or get out of hand. They do not just hold others accountable, but they do the same with themselves.

Mindful leaders are considerate in their communications. They regularly appreciate the contributions of their workforce. Their workers are attuned to hear critical or not-so-positive messages constructively. These leaders organize their communications in a truthful, beneficial, not-disturbing and pleasing manner. They are thoughtful of how they communicate. And they do so with the view to inspire the individuals to do and give more.

Finally, mindful leaders are transformational in the way they think and behave. They love commitment, training, and work. Their efforts cannot be measured in one dimension. Company profits are not the real result but evidence of a healthy team behind them. They urge individuals need to evaluate their emotions and become more self-aware. They bring their team to their optimal personal routines that foster individual engagement, efficiency, productivity, and progress quickly.

Organizations know that mindful leaders work through greater retention because they think of others. Individuals are happier at work. They are being recognized for their efforts. They work through established positive relationships amongst themselves. Conflicts and tensions are resolved more humanly than systematically. Their energy and optimism are contagious because they are each clear with their purposes both at the workplace and in their personal lives.

Chapter 8:

Exercises for Leading with Emotional Intelligence

When we become self-aware, we know what we are doing as we do it and understand why we are doing it. To be self-aware is to be conscious and ably monitor what goes on while keeping out awareness of the nature and quality happenings, and well discerning their meanings. When we are not conscious, we unconsciously fall short of our self-awareness.

As a leader, you want to live above subconscious biases and blind spots that you naturally have as a human. Humanly speaking the confidence that we hold in self-knowledge often no justify us to be right. It turns out our self-awareness does not match up to the levels we think. Self-awareness is a skill that is also learned through stages. Humans are naturally subconsciously incompetent. We never imagine how poor at something we normally are when we are starting out at it. Similarly, we are mistaken to think that we already really know ourselves without having worked at it.

Incompetence causes discomfort when someone is trying to do something new and it may make them avoid learning it altogether. This is the kind of discomfort that persists during learning self-awareness and it makes many people go through life without developing it. Like you work to build any other skill, developing awareness of self requires that you employ the right methods and consistently keep practicing.

Building self-awareness is a process that works to strengthen your conscious connection to all the three brain regions. Different activities strengthen the connections in different brain parts. Ultimately you work at it to gain more consciousness what drives your behavior. As a leader, your sensitivity to emotions and instincts needs to be elevated beyond the normal. You will rarely access this kind of information through your conscious mind alone. It is an empowerment for you to explore your thoughts, your beliefs, and your biases with greater outcomes.

Self-awareness starts from your center. Centering is the first step in learning self-awareness because it serves to increase attention: essential for you to learn, understand, and develop in any other area. Meditation will help you gain a unique perspective on your life experiences. Observational meditation creates a space between your actions, and your thoughts, and your feelings. Over and over, the observing self begins to monitor your thoughts and the accompanying feelings and resultant actions with objectivity.

This observing self is not born with us; we develop it. It then helps us to develop our self-awareness. The development of self-awareness is integral in reconnecting with your body and instincts with the view to foster and fortify body and mind connection.

Exercises for Self-Awareness

i. Mindful Meditation

Becoming truly aware of yourself starts at establishing your center and connecting on a deeper level with your mind. And finding the 'center' of your being is most effectively achieved through meditation. The benefits of meditation and their importance on your emotional and psychological health are many and profound. You practice mindful meditation by placing your mind in a more restful state, and then become more conscious of yourself, your emotions, and your personality.

ii. Connect with Purpose

Pay close conscious attention to the things that you do and consider by yourself what you do them for, for whom you do them - you or someone else, the long and short term intents of doing them, and whether in that moment they matter the most in alignment with your life purposes.

Take note of everything and every action you undertake on a daily basis and establish the reasons you do them for.

Identify what is most important among them and invest most of your time in it. This way you will become better at focusing and knowing yourself.

iii. Revisit Your Values

If you notice that you are spending most of your time at the wrong things or for the wrong reasons then be sure that some things are definitely not seated right and that they do not resonate with your purposes and beliefs.

Develop your values and beliefs as deeply engrained in you and use them to keep your action list in check. Find where there are discrepancies, and establish the reasons for them. Your focus will be greatly improved.

iv. Reflect on Your Feelings

Take your necessary time to understand and reflect on what you are feeling. We barely ever do that.

Write down your emotions, either in the moment or later in the day by trying to reactivate it-- agitation, joy, anger, sadness, etc., and get it to the next level by describing the emotion using a metaphor.

v. Keep an Emotions Journal

Take time to think about the emotions you feel in the day and how they can help you to understand yourself better.

In the evening, create two columns on each page: emotions in the left listed by the hour, and context that surrounded that emotion in the right.

Compare and analyze the ratio of positive versus negative emotions and note the dominant emotions and their causes along with their triggers.

This will enable you to point exactly where your emotions come from so that you can begin to work on transmuting their triggers and hence, bringing to an end the invoking of negative emotions thereby minimizing their effects.

vi.   SWOT Analysis

Do an analysis of yourself, your life, your feelings and emotions, and your overall welfare in your most convenient terms starting with a SWOT analysis. SWOT stands for strengths, weaknesses, opportunities, and threats. Entrepreneurs often include SWOT analysis in business proposals. You can apply the same principles towards your self-study. Analyze your strengths in terms of natural endowment and acquired skill and weaknesses – insufficiency of skill and resources, and then the opportunities you perceive being available for your growth versus any potential threats to your capability to progress towards your objectives.

vii.   You Are Human

Do not put too much undue pressure on yourself. Life is never absolutely perfect and mistakes are an accepted part of it. Everyone suffers from different problems. By recognizing your problems, you begin to create the capability to determine the most appropriate solutions for them.

viii.   Three Why's

People still find it appropriate to apply this old theory in their own lives. Whenever a problem arises, ask why on the first round, and establish the reasons. For each of the reasons found, ask why, and develop a second level of the reasons then subsequently like that. You will know when to stop when you can no longer get worthwhile answers for the question. The formulate solution at that stage. It often goes three steps deep but it can go even more or less depending on the nature of the problem.

ix.   Take responsibility

Learn to forgive yourself when you experience failure in your ventures. Importantly at the same time, you must take responsibility for your thoughts and actions. Step up and man up to the things that you are accountable for. Do not blame your own failures, errors, and mistakes on other people. Take responsibility and you will be better able to embrace the opportunities for learning and feel lots better at the end.

x. Keep a Journal

Most people do not really regard the idea of carrying a journal with them as appropriate. But you need to have one and as much as possible keep contributing to it. However, it provides a fundamental means for you to monitor yourself, and the thoughts, successes, and failures you experience. This needs to become a significant part of you in your journey of inner discovery of self. Analyze it daily, and see how more aware of who you become and how you can improve.

xi. Sacrifice to Become Successful

Journeying to a conscious self-awareness and elevated level of success requires certain shorter-term sacrifices to guarantee the achievement of your longer-term goals. You must say no to certain habits that are counter-productive to your main goals. They are short term losses that can pay off big time later in life.

xii. Breathe Before You Speak

Make it your norm to take deep breaths and analyze situations before you speak on an aggravating or frustrating problem. This will help to alleviate the severity of your reactions to the problem by taking a moment to formulate a better solution, even if temporary, to the problem at hand.

xiii. Seek Feedback

It is not entirely effective to assess your own behaviors and other traits and affirm them you're your perspectives alone. Obtain honest feedback from people who have your values and objectives at heart. Feedback is feedback, even if negative sometimes, as long as you find something constructive about it for your development.

xiv.   Watch Your Progress

However, much you do, also watch your progress towards self-awareness to ensure you are making real progress. Importantly too, take some time every regularly to reflect on the progress you are making.

Exercises for Self-Management

i.   Breathe

We are ever so busy these days that we rarely afford ourselves moments to take enough breaths we deserve.

In instances of stress, step back, then close your eyes and take some breaths for a few moments. Feel them and the experience of it. Monitor yourself in the course of it while withholding your situational default reaction. Loosen your mind for a bit and get to resume when you feel your state of calmness return and your thought process is straight.

ii.   Count to Ten

When you are under stress, take a step back as well as breathe and also count to ten slowly. Breathe in slowly and count as you exhale and then do this ten times. Taking sips of water before enacting or pronouncing things help avoid snapping as well as allow you to calm down.

iii.   Reframe

Everyone perceives things differently. What is good for one is not so for the other. Change how you view things, especially when under stress or are angered and you will better manage your emotions in the situation. You can do this by either of the following two ways.

Reframe your context; compare with any other situations in which this action or behavior would be positive, for instance, someone's excessive stubbornness. This great skill is required when you experience a tough time in which ordinarily by yourself you cannot suffice.

Reframe your content: ask yourself if there can be another positive meaning of the happening or behavior, for instance, what you stand to gain by just missing the bus.

The idea to give your mind a chance to perceive reality, even in the worst moments, and out of that serve youth best way possible.

iv.   Create Time for Learning Problem-Solving

You never find time to think about or through things by strictly heeding to a constantly busy schedule that is full of packed or overlapping activities. To become creative at solving problems, you have to dedicate the time for that over and above the time you spend doing your other regular or routine assignments.

Dedicate 15 minutes a day in your calendar to be reflecting and thinking as you take a walk. This practice will prepare your mind and thinking to handle situations in your best, possible desired way that is known to you prior.

v.   Improve Your Bed Hygiene

You might be guilty of this —having your laptop with you in bed, your kindle, your phone, your tablet, and many other gadgets to keep you busy therein.

Learn to disconnect from these devices more often and generally decide to leave them out of the bedroom. Ideally, you need to want to turn off the laptop or TV two hours before you retire to bed; their light persists in the brains for a while even after you close your eyes, delaying sleep. Sufficient sleep is important for your proper physical and mental functioning.

vi.   Always Live in The Moment

Are you the kind that prefers to multi-task all the time in managing all your duties that you, most likely, force upon yourself? Try the following.

- When in a meeting, let it just that: observing the attendants, listening to their inputs, your gadgets shut; be only just in that meeting.
- Just only eat, when eating. No mail compositions or replies or texting and messaging but, maybe exceptionally, do speak only so much with the people around.
- Attend to the phone call exclusively: not emailing at the same time, or chatting, studying reports, or deciding between options, or whatever else.
- Do not be busy with other things while having dinner with others. Only focus on the conversation you are having.

In whatever situation, avoid thinking about things of the past or contemplating about the future, and focus on that moment presently and exclusively. Strive to fully experience the now and here. You lead a better life by recognizing and appreciating people present and getting a full experience of the moments at hand.

vii.   Take a 15-Minute Tour Around

Have you ever considered how much your mind gets stuck within until you totally disconnect with the worlds around you? There is just so much you can learn from out there.

So, whether at your office, at home, or at an event, take moments to observe the behavior around you. Observe the time when people walk around and go conversing and with whom they converse, their moods, the arrangements of their desks, what they feel, their general attitude, what they display and what they say. Do it daily with a neutral clear intention to learn about and of the people and things around you.

viii.   Watch People

It is interesting what watching people, their interactions, feelings and attitudes, foods and how they eat, body language and cues, their expressions of faces, etc. can tell you about human behaviors. It will influence your skills of empathy and improve your ability to discern people.

ix.   Develop A Back-Pocket Question

Have you ever fallen into an awkward situation when you met someone new and you had to have a conversation and didn't know how to break that silence when the conversation seemed to be dropping? Always have an open question that you can ask to have them open up and share their opinion on an issue or something. The conversation will then begin to pick up again from there.

x.   The Least is the Great

Do not keep forgetting that the small things really count as over-time, they constitute the whole. Always remember to have etiquette, show courtesy and gratitude and generally be open, positive, friendly, and receptive. Say "thank you," "please," and "I'm sorry." Consciously invest in this, and do not deny it. They form the foundation for enduring relations with other people.

Also, as many times as possible, say people's names. Everyone likes to hear their name. So, handle it as that important. It evokes nice feelings in people.

xi.   Show You Care, When You Do

You could be guilty of the presumption that people generally know that you love them and expect them to deduce and feel it by reading your attitudes. But it does not happen like that. When caring about someone for who they are or what they do, say it, and show that and offer gestures of gratitude and great feeling for them. Little gifts personalized for the recipients are quite memorable and will be remembered till long after.

xii.   Do Not Just Make Decisions, Explain Them

This is very important especially for leadership at the workplace. A leadership that just decides at things and hopes for everyone to be agreeable often finds it almost impossible to bring the rest of the team on board. People want to know the reasons behind decisions. When they understand it better, they get along with it better.

Change of management, for instance, affects the workers and they need to make relevant adjustments in time so as to create a smooth efficient transition. People do not just accept things; the options that were available, and how a particular one is settled, and how everyone is affected. The same principle applies to your personal life with family and friends.

xiii.   Tackle tough conversations

Confrontations are all-feared for. The same is the case with discussions that are critical in nature. But they always occur to stir up progress. One approach toward them is as follows:

- Start by establishing an initial shared ground on the problem
- Listen to the other opinions
- Be patient, listen for understanding of your counterpart, without defending yourself on the go
- Assist them understand you by describing to them your discomforts, thoughts, ideas, reasons, etc.
- Formulate a bearable solution based on everyone's contributions
- Agree on the implementation framework and commit to the process
- Review and check in on progress made regularly and enact any adjustments if necessary

This approach ensures that everyone understands how they contributed toward a situation and therefore consider what they have to do to restore things to normal. The objective is, beyond solving the primary problem at hand, to also reinforce the relationship between the two of you going forward.

In a closing note, consider to also undertake your regular bodily exercise. All forms of good exercise help to create and restore energy into you, improve your concentration ability, improve your resistance, enhance your confidence, keep you inspired, encourages self-improvement, heighten your balance, improve your creativity and decision-making, and encourage your coordination capabilities.

Self-awareness is an observer for behaviors and facilitator of enhanced understanding of intentions and self. The right combination of methodology and regular exercise help build awareness of self. Employ various activities and exercises and your physical, emotional, and psychological balance will function in sync. The exercises listed above offer an integrated approach by which you can cultivate true self-awareness.

There is no better feeling that you will get as a leader than knowing that you are being true to yourself and to your team in everything you do.

Conclusion

This book has deeply discussed the various issues around emotional intelligence. The goal has been to help you align better with the ideal personality and temperament that makes a successful leader. The whole point that has run across the book is that we cannot embody the personalities of successful leaders if we are not able to control the pressure in us, the conflicts in our lives, and the emotional storms that could burst out in certain circumstances.

In Chapter One, we discussed how emotions are sensed, and even experienced. This could help us be more aware of ourselves. You have to know the process that sets you on an emotional path. This way, you will be in a better position to monitor yourself and regulate your emotions.

In that regard, the book gives you various ways of ensuring you exercise self-regulation. Emotions should not be left to spin out of control. The self-regulation chapter explains this and provides you with the avenues and options that you have that could help you in your self-regulation efforts.

This book even makes you realize that emotions can be purposefully experienced. They can be used in a focused way that does not malign our character, particularly in the place where we are supposed to lead. This is explained in great detail in the book, and from that point, you start to master your emotions not as a threat, but as an asset.

For leaders, interpersonal skills are also a vital set of skills to have. This means that one has to ensure that emotions do not come in the way of creating meaningful interactions. How this can be achieved is all laid out for you.

Even more important is that the book prepares you to maneuver the challenges of leadership. This is particularly with regard to the resistance you may have to confront particularly in the role of a change manager. This can test your emotional triggers and hence it is better to be ahead of yourself on the same in order to be prepared to deal with others starting from dealing with yourself.

The exercises for emotional intelligence are the real deal of making you acquire the intelligence. They are explained in an easy way with relevance to the leadership challenges that the entire book has been identifying. This culminates in a guiding emotional intelligence guidebook that you definitely have loved reading.

www.ingramcontent.com/pod-product-compliance
Lightning Source LLC
Chambersburg PA
CBHW070348220526
45467CB00001B/289